D0983029

MEMOIRS OF
A HAPPY FAILURE

Memoirs of a
Happy Failure

Alice von Hildebrand

with John Henry Crosby

Foreword by *Timothy Cardinal Dolan*

SAINT BENEDICT ✛ PRESS
Charlotte, North Carolina

Cataloging-in-Publication data on file with the Library of Congress.

Interior design by Ryan Scheife.
Cover design by Marylouise McGraw

ISBN: 978-1-61890-126-2

Published in the United States by Saint Benedict Press, LLC
PO Box 410487 Charlotte, NC 28241
www.SaintBenedictPress.com

Printed and bound in the United States of America.

MORE PRAISE FOR
MEMOIRS OF A HAPPY FAILURE

"In the history of traditional Catholicism in the late 20th century, there are many unsung heroes. I know of only one who refers to herself as a happy failure. Those who know Alice von Hildebrand know she is truly happy; but she is far from a failure. She is not only the great woman behind the great man—her renowned husband Dietrich—she is also a brilliant philosopher who has continued Dietrich's work and has brought generations of her students to realize the evils of moral relativism and the beauty of revealed truth. In this delightful self-effacing account of her struggles and triumphs in secular academia, her absence of failure is here for all to see. I simply loved this entertaining and inspiring little book."

—HON. ANDREW P. NAPOLITANO, SENIOR JUDICIAL ANALYST,
FOX NEWS CHANNEL

"Dr. Alice von Hildebrand is a woman both ahead of her time in her achievements and timeless in her commitment to defending truth. Her story, and the conversion stories of her students, remind us that the very convictions that bring worldly reproach can be the ones God uses to touch hearts, change lives and save souls."

— COLLEEN CARROLL CAMPBELL, AUTHOR OF
MY SISTERS, THE SAINTS AND *THE NEW FAITHFUL*

"Ours is an age in desperate need for courageous witness to the truth, with integrity and grace. Lily Hildebrand provides just such a witness, chronicling with first-hand experience the siege under which that truth nevertheless prevails."

—FRANK HANNA, CEO OF HANNA CAPITAL,
AND FOUNDER OF THE SOLIDARITY ASSOCIATION

"Alice von Hildebrand's memoirs are the breathtaking account of one of the Great Catholic women academics of this and the last century. I can't wait for the movie.

—FATHER C. J. MCCLOSKEY III, STD,
PRIEST OF THE PRELATURE OF OPUS DEI AN
RESEARCH FELLOW OF THE FAITH AND REASON INSTITUTE

"This is a life singularly blessed with friendship and adventure, dazzling in its singularity. Yet it is full of lessons for all readers. Though our lives may not have the cinematic scope and sweep of Dr. von Hildebrand's, they have no less drama in spiritual terms. She models a fierce courage of mind and heart that we would do well to imitate. Our own friendships and adventures can be far richer because we read this book."

—MICHAEL AQUILINA, EWTN HOST AND AUTHOR OF
A YEAR WITH THE CHURCH FATHERS

"Just as she is herself, Alice von Hildebrand's memoir of her years at Hunter College is a glistering, brilliant, priceless gem. She is so witty, wise, and indefatigable in her stand for Truth that simply to be in her presence, whether in the classroom or in the vital pages of this book, is to be profoundly inspired. I am only grieved it is not much longer and sorry it wasn't published years ago. Her voice is a matchless gift: edifying, galvanizing, and wildly entertaining."

—ERIC METAXAS, *NEW YORK TIMES* BESTSELLING AUTHOR OF
BONHOEFFER: PASTOR, MARTYR, PROPHET, SPY
AND HOST OF SOCRATES IN THE CITY

"*Memoirs of a Happy Failure* fills us with gratitude for the gift of Dr. Alice von Hildebrand's life in Christ, lived with so much integrity and vigor over many years, as she has tirelessly given witness to the truth by both her example and her teaching. Especially noteworthy are the chapters of her memoirs which treat the challenges she faced during her thirty-seven years of teaching at Hunter College. Amidst the often difficult challenges, she experienced the incomparable blessing of students inspired, through the knowledge of truth gained in her philosophy courses, to seek Him who is Truth and to receive the gift of faith in Christ Who alone is our salvation. Dr. von Hildebrand was a highly competent professor, who truly loved her students and, therefore, rejoiced, above all, when they came to the truth at its living source in God – Father, Son, and Holy Spirit. I am confident that *Memoirs of a Happy Failure*, by which Dr. Alice von Hildebrand recounts her life and work as a philosopher, will encourage the reader, and particularly all teachers, to be steadfast in speaking and living "the truth in love" (Cf. Eph 4:15)."

—HIS EMINENCE RAYMOND LEO CARDINAL BURKE,
PREFECT OF THE APOSTOLIC SIGNATURA

"Thanks are due to the distinguished philosopher and theologian Alice von Hildebrand for this illuminating glimpse into her joys and struggles as a woman and a Catholic over four eventful decades in the American academic world. Her love of truth shines forth on every page of this fascinating personal Memoir."

—Mary Ann GLENDON, LEARNED HAND PROFESSOR OF LAW,
HARVARD UNIVERSITY

"This intimate, poignant memoir demonstrates the power of placing one's trust in God and therein finding the strength to endure suffering and transform lives. Lily Von Hildebrand has done just that. She is a treasure, and her story a must-read."

—RAYMOND ARROYO, *NEW YORK TIMES* BEST SELLING AUTHOR OF
MOTHER ANGELICA AND THE KERMAN DERMAN CHRONICLES.
EWTN NEWS MANAGING EDITOR.

~

*To my dear friends, Fr. Benedict Groeschel, CFR
and Mother Mary Angelica, PCPA
whose lives have been guided by two golden truths:*

"Without me you can do nothing." (John 15:5)

*"I can do all things through Him who strengthens me."
(Phil 4:13)*

FOREWORD

We all appreciate the impact made by a great teacher. In fact, you can probably think of the ways in which a few extraordinary teachers influenced your own development. Such a memorable teacher did not just impart knowledge of a given subject to you, but rather inspired you in some way to continue striving for truth. Ultimately, we know that Truth is not a *what* , but a *who*, that is, the person of Jesus Christ from whom all truth originates, who called Himself, "The Truth." Whether the subject is philosophy, history, theology—even geometry—a great teacher shows us the beauty of truth and knowledge, the ultimate goal of education.

Dr. Alice von Hildebrand has achieved many things in her life, but her memoirs reveal that throughout the many trials and triumphs she has always remained a dedicated teacher devoted to pointing her students toward the saving Truth of Jesus Christ.

Dr. von Hildebrand has faced many obstacles along the way: from fleeing the Nazi menace in her youth; to the challenge of gaining a foothold as a philosophy professor in what was then a male-dominated profession; to the often-hostile ideological battles she faced as an increasingly rare witness to the existence of objective truth. Yet, as I read her account of these episodes, I did not find bitterness, but rather a quiet confidence that God's grace has helped her through these difficulties. There it is: great teachers not only impart wisdom in the classroom; the example of their life often provides an even more valuable lesson.

Of course there is more to Dr. von Hildebrand than just her excellent career as a professor at Hunter College here in New York City. She was a devoted and loving wife to her late and legendary husband Dietrich, and her tireless efforts to promote the legacy of this great Catholic thinker are nothing short of remarkable. Since her retirement she has also written several books, a fact which is omitted in her memoirs on account of her characteristic modesty. These books carry her insights and knowledge beyond the lecture hall, and we are all fortunate that her "retirement" has yielded such an impressive output of writing! As you read these memoirs I am sure that you, like me, will learn many things. What else should we expect from such an accomplished teacher? But I hope that Dr. von Hildebrand's fascinating life also brings into sharp relief the way in which all people—whether their title is Cardinal, Professor, Mom, Dad, or Friend—are called to bring the light of Christ into the word around them. The stories recounted here of the transformative impact that God's love had on so many of Dr. von Hildebrand's students remind us that we are all instruments of God's plan. And that is a great lesson for us all.

Timothy Michael Cardinal Dolan
Archbishop of New York
June 24, 2014

PREFACE

I must have been about three or four years old. Our family was on vacation at my parents' summer house in Duinbergen on the Belgian coast. Roaming about the sandy hills, I came across a bush that triggered my curiosity and bending toward it, to my enchantment, I discovered a nest. The blessing of being a child is that one lives in a constant state of awe, the famous philosophical "wondering," so highly praised by the Greeks. Woe to the nation whose children can no longer wonder.

I recall looking at it again and again. There was a masterpiece of nature made up of small, insignificant twigs that the bird's beak had woven together into a kind of organic work of art. It was beautiful. How right Plato was when he wrote that at the sight of beauty the human soul grows wings. I was awed, and had a taste of real happiness, so very different from the pleasure I experienced while eating delicious Belgian chocolates.

Then I came closer to the nest, where to my horror, I saw a dead chick. It was my first encounter with death, and even though so young, I grasped in some vague fashion that it was a terrible punishment. I started sobbing uncontrollably, and ran to my mother for comfort.

The memory of this little nest and the dead chick came to me suddenly as I was re-reading these memoirs of mine.

God in His Wisdom does not show us the whole way

we have to travel. How many of us would turn back, if we only knew what was awaiting us. I thank Him for not having revealed to me how arduous my task would be: to hold high the flag in defense of the objectivity of truth in a fortress of relativism.

From one point of view, the episodes that make up the story of my life are small, insignificant twigs—many of which were prickly. But, like that nest I saw nearly eighty-seven years ago, God has woven a beautiful nest out of the "twigs" of my life.

CHAPTER 1

In the wee hours of Tuesday, June 11, 1940, I was awakened by the ringing of the ship's bells. I tiptoed to open the door of our cabin and to my amazement saw people in pajamas and nightgowns with life-preservers around their waists, rushing toward the deck. I immediately woke my sister, Louloute (pronounced "Loo-lute"). The two Russian ladies who shared our cabin went to find out what was happening. They returned with upsetting news. Our vessel, the SS Washington, had been intercepted by a German U-boat. We had been given one hour to board our lifeboats and put out to sea. Our ship would then be torpedoed.

Louloute and I hastily donned our summer dresses (it is strange what the mind recalls, but I remember that mine was navy blue with polka dots), grabbed our pocketbooks, and left the cabin. It is also extraordinary that at a time of such anxiety, I was very observant and had noticed already on the day we boarded the *Washington* that in case of an emergency, we were supposed to go to lifeboat number ten. There was enormous tension. People were pushing and pressing up the narrow staircase, and my one fear was to be separated from my beloved sister, for at that moment she was everything to me. I locked my arm in hers and was mainly concerned about her welfare, as she easily got upset. I even tried a bit of humor. "I have forgotten my toothbrush," I quipped.

When we arrived on deck, we discovered that lifeboat ten was filled to capacity. The captain had issued orders that only women and children could board the boats, as there were far more passengers than lifeboats. But there were some men in the lifeboats that had ignored the order because their wives insisted they accompany them.

We found ourselves on deck, looking out onto the mysterious, fog-covered Atlantic. I was convinced I was about to die and that soon I would be facing God. It was then that I had one of the most extraordinary experiences of my life. With a clarity and precision that approached the supernatural, all of a sudden, in a single flash, I relived everything I had ever done, failed to do, thought, imagined, and felt. The experience was overwhelming, and convinced me of God's goodness. Could I not assume that, at the very moment of death, God would grant this experience to everyone, so that each person would have the chance to say, "Have mercy on me, my Lord"? This experience had such an impact on me that I believe I went from youth to maturity in a few brief instants. I had the clear sense that I had "touched eternity," where time vanishes and everything is present.

I survived this brush with death, but my instantaneous maturing was a grace that prepared me for what lay ahead. Had someone told me that I would spend most of my life in the United States, and earn my living teaching philosophy at a secular university, where I would suffer nearly four decades of endless efforts to undermine and deter my teaching, my response would have been one of total disbelief coupled with dread. Nothing in my sheltered background had prepared me for this.

But as I look back on my life of nine decades, I see the providence of God in everything. Not only did He sustain me with His grace, He gave me the great gift of many beautiful friendships and above all my marriage to Dietrich von Hildebrand, that knight for truth and ardent lover of the Church. My years as a professor of philosophy were at times harrowing and difficult, but thanks to the deep sense of mission I felt toward my students, I was able to find joy and serenity even in the darkest times.

There comes a moment when a story like mine must be told. Indeed, it is a necessary act of gratitude. My life has been like a novel, sometimes with a Dostoevsky note, when I consider the cast of characters.

CHAPTER 2

To grasp the shock I experienced upon arriving in America, I need to say a word about my youth, for I was—and continue to be—deeply shaped by my upbringing. I was born and raised in Belgium, that small and beautiful country so deeply marked by Catholic culture. Its churches, the numerous small chapels that greeted me on walks in the magnificent forest of Soignes that surrounds Brussels, its superb paintings (van Eyck and Memling spring to mind), the ringing of the carillon that delighted me when we passed through Bruges on our way to the seashore where my parents had a summer home; all were a reminder that the meaning of human life is to serve God in this life and to enjoy Him forever in the next.

My youth was sheltered. My father Henri, a daily communicant, sent his children to the very best schools. My brother was educated by the Jesuits at the Collège Saint-Michel in Brussels while my sisters (one older and two younger) and I attended the Berlaymont, run by the Canonesses of Saint Augustine, and located a hundred yards from the house in which I was born. The nuns, many of them aristocrats, had fled France when Georges Clémenceau, the fiercely anti-clerical prime minister during the early 1900s, closed many French convents.

My paternal grandfather, Louis Jourdain, was a brilliant engineer whose talent and training took him to

England and Romania. He was the youngest of ten children, and very attached to his family. When he learned that his brother, Victor, ten years his senior with a wife and several children to support, had gone bankrupt, he offered to contribute his entire salary until all his brother's debts had been paid, in exchange for only room and board. The honor of the family had to be vindicated.

After completing this labor of love, Louis decided to get married. (He, over forty at the time, and his fiancée, Alice Sorel, only twenty-five.) So it came about that my great-uncle Victor's last child was a few months older than my grandfather's first, a daughter named Laure. She was followed by four sons: Léon, Henri (my father), Pierre, and Robert (who became a Jesuit).

Though Belgium was a Catholic country, surprisingly enough, it had no Catholic newspaper. Understanding the power of the press, my grandfather and his brother felt it to be their mission to make up for this deficiency. They wanted to help nourish the Belgian population with the fullness of Catholic teaching, dogmatic as well as moral and social, and so they founded Le Patriote (The Patriot) in 1883. Since Victor's bankruptcy had put his name under a cloud, only my grandfather's name appeared as a founder. This is how the newspaper that would come to play such an important role in Belgium was begun.*

The paper was an immediate success because it responded to a real need. Victor and Louis were disciplined,

---

* Before founding Le Patriote, Louis had made the discovery of important carbon deposits in the Belgian Limburg region. Though retaining fifty percent of its stocks, he chose not to have these mines named after him because of his involvement with the newspaper, naming them after a close associate, André Dumont.

hard-working, and deeply Catholic. *Le Patriote* swept the country and many years later in Rome when I visited Cardinal Oddi (who had been nuncio in Brussels), he dubbed it "the most Catholic newspaper in the world." (Alas, it was sold in the 1970s, and that is no longer the case.)

In 1914, when Belgium was invaded by Germany, the brothers closed the newspaper for fear it would be used as a tool for German propaganda. Despite shuttering their operations, they paid all their employees for the rest of the war to prevent them from being forced to work in German war factories in order to feed their families. My great-uncle Victor then started an underground newspaper called *La Libre Belgique* (*Free Belgium*),* which succeeded in keeping up the morale of Belgians severely tried by the brutality of the Germans. Entertaining and witty, it made fun of the "*Boches,*" as the German occupiers were pejoratively called. To the joy of the Belgian people, it was published throughout the whole war. Each issue was published by a different printer and distributed at night, a tactic that prevented the Germans from discovering the paper's operations.

I am reminded of a lovely example of the wit of the Belgians, namely the trick they played on the Germans on the occasion of the Belgian Day of Independence (July 21). The Germans had prohibited any patriotic manifesta-

---

* In her Pulitzer Prize-winning book, *The Guns of August* (New York: MacMillan, 1962), 173, Barbara Tuchman mistakenly refers to the newspaper as *Le Libre Belge* (The Free Belgian). In a letter of congratulations to Tuchman, I gently pointed out that the newspaper had been called *La Libre Belgique*, noting that I was the grandniece of Victor Jourdain and granddaughter of Louis Jourdain. I received a terse reply: I checked my files and my information is correct. Alas, she missed the subtle double play on meanings: a defiant claim to Belgian freedom coupled with an appeal to free Belgium from the German oppressors.

tion and in their bad French accents said, "*tout ouvert*," (everything should be kept open), which the witty Belgians transformed into "*tout tout vert*" (everything should be green). Dutifully obeying the German command, everyone donned green clothing. The Germans, who entirely missed the joke, feared that some sort of revolt was being planned and doubled the number of soldiers commanding key positions in Brussels. Needless to say, the Belgians were enjoying themselves immensely.

There is supreme irony in the fact that the Germans conducted an unannounced search on Victor's house just as he was penning an article for *La Libre Belgique*. Speaking in a commanding and authoritative tone that admitted of no reply, he said, "Look wherever you please, but do not disturb me. I am a very busy man." And he peacefully continued to write the article that was to be published the next morning. Thus he deflected attention from his work of resistance, which was carried out in the very presence of the Germans! Both brothers died just before the end of the war, and then, at the request of Cardinal Mercier, *Le Patriote* was revived under the name of *La Libre Belgique*.

Alas, the political clear-sightedness of my grandfather and great-uncle was not shared in equal measure by all members of their family. Being ardent Belgian patriots, one can only imagine their grief that my father's brother, Léon Jourdain and his wife Claire were pro-Boches. Naturally, they had to be kept in the dark about La Libre Belgique during World War I. Léon never suspected that his uncle, and indirectly his family, were involved with the famous underground paper.

Through my mother, I am a van de Vorst. My maternal

grandfather, Albert, was a maritime lawyer by profession at a time when Antwerp was the third largest harbor in the world. He was, I was told, one of three or four of the most prominent maritime lawyers of his day. He was a radical liberal, as was, for the most part, the entire van de Vorst family. The noteworthy exception was my great-uncle, Fr. Charles van de Vorst, S. J., who became Provincial of the Jesuits in Belgium and later assistant to the worldwide head of the Jesuit order in Rome known as the "Black Pope". When the head of the Jesuits, Fr. Wlodimir Ledóchowski, S. J., died in 1942, it was impossible to hold an election for a new superior general because of the war. I was told that Fr. Charles was on top of the list of candidates to succeed him. When the election was finally held in 1946, he was seventy-six and no longer eligible for the office. But his closest friend, Fr. Jean-Baptiste Janssens, S. J. was elected and called my uncle to Rome to serve as his assistant where he died in 1955.

My father and mother could not have come from more different backgrounds. As a result there was a great deal of tension between their families: in short, they were not compatible. The Jourdains had the reputation (thanks in large part to my grandfather) for being sound, traditional Catholics, while the van de Vorsts were quite liberal (again, with the exception of my great-uncle Fr. Charles).

I came to the United States with my older sister, Marie Hélène (nicknamed Louloute) as a refugee in 1940. My father's sister, Laure, and her husband, Robert Brunner, had emigrated to the US in the fall of 1939 because they foresaw that war was inevitable and imminent. My uncle had headed a bank in Brussels, and decided to leave so as to save the assets of his clients (many of whom belonged to the French clergy). My aunt and uncle left Rotterdam in September and settled at the Waldorf Astoria in New York City, where they lived for many years. He maintained an office at Brown Brothers Harriman, one of the most prestigious private banks on Wall Street. I knew my aunt and uncle very little. We did pay them a yearly visit at Christmas and on New Year's, and received generous gifts for the Feast of Saint Nicholas, which is much celebrated in Belgium. From time to time, my aunt would invite us for tea at her magnificent property in Boitsfort on the outskirts of Brussels. Louloute, however, knew them much better, as my aunt and uncle had taken an interest in her when she was fifteen. She struck them as frail and anemic and in need of care. Having convinced themselves that I tended toward the van de Vorst side of the family, Louloute seemed physically to resemble my aunt, and so they "adopted" her, paying for physical examinations and for several-weeks vacations to a lovely spa on the Belgian seashore to build up her health. My uncle in particular took a great liking to her, as she was very pretty and feminine. My aunt spent much of her time in bed—I never found out what her ailment was—and often retreated to the famous spa of Valmont in the mountains above Geneva. My uncle was a passionate traveler, and, as they had no children, Louloute was invited to accompany him to Switzerland and Italy on one occasion, and on another to join him on a Mediterranean cruise, with stops in Egypt, Syria, and Greece.

The political situation, however, had become so threatening that my uncle cancelled the next trip he had planned with her, and at that point in 1939 decided to emigrate for the duration of the war, offering to take Louloute with them. My father refused—something I found out only much later.

In 1940 Louloute suggested to my aunt and uncle that we visit them in New York City for a span of three weeks. They accepted her proposal and my efficient uncle immediately booked tickets on the SS Manhattan that was leaving from Genoa on June 2. My uncle found out that his friend, Robert Lovett, the future Secretary of Defense under Truman, was traveling on the Manhattan and asked him to look out for us. The situation changed radically when war broke out. Belgium was invaded by the Nazis on Friday, May 10, 1940. I still remember my father rushing into my bedroom at five in the morning to tell me that the Germans had attacked. We could hear bombing in the distance.

After consulting with his younger brother, Fr. Robert Jourdain, S. J., my father decided that the family should leave the country and get to Southern France, as far away from the Germans as possible. We hurriedly left Brussels by car on Sunday, May 12, with a contingent of Jesuits, spread over several vehicles. My older sister and I spent one night in Tronchiennes, close to Ghent, where my great-uncle Fr. Charles van de Vorst, S. J., found us a place to stay overnight; we then joined my parents (whose car had not been stopped for control by soldiers) at their house in Duinbergen on the Belgian coast. From there we went to Tournai, close to the French border. That night we heard the explosions of the nearby blitzkrieg. We waited twenty-four hours at the French border, which had been shut to refugees, until the French reopened the border the following day.

That night we arrived in Beaumont west of Paris where we unwittingly slept in a brothel: all the hotels were booked

to capacity, given the frightful flow of refugees fleeing south-
ward from Holland and Belgium. Our itinerary was set by
the Jesuits, always aiming at towns with a Jesuit house.

The entire next night was spent on the road. We rested
for a couple of days in Moulins, and then, passing through
Clermont-Ferrand, arrived in Bordeaux and rented a few
rooms in a very modest, flea-infested house, which by then
was all that was available. Louloute and I no longer wanted
to leave our parents for an unknown period of time. But
when rumors began to spread that Nazi soldiers were rap-
ing young girls on their "glorious blitzkrieg," the question
of our departure was seriously considered. My father, bom-
barded by telegrams from my uncle in the US, agreed to
let us leave. He sent us to the American consulate, where
a large poster indicated that only American citizens would
be granted admittance. We relayed this information to my
father, who cabled my uncle that getting American visas
was out of the question. But the latter, being a very wealthy
man with connections in the financial world, went straight
to the State Department in Washington, D.C., and managed to have them send a telegram to the consul in Bordeaux ordering him to grant us visas. Our presence was
requested by the Department of State: a glorious beginning! How many can boast this distinction? I learned that
money is a powerful tool. I also learned that God had His
mysterious plans. This was indeed a strange beginning.

On Thursday, June 6, the consul sent a bellboy to our
address in Bordeaux, which I still remember: 14 Rue de la
Course. My father was "at home," while my mother and
her four daughters were in a nearby park where, I distinctly
recall, my youngest sister, aged four, was happily feeding the

ducks. When we heard the news, we rushed over to the consulate, which was being kept open for our sake, and in a few moments were granted those precious papers. The next difficulty was that we had no Belgian passports, having left home in such a topsy-turvy fashion, and the Belgian consul was prohibited from granting them by his government. But America is a powerful country and the American consul *ordered* the Belgian consul to grant us passports immediately, to which the Belgian consul retorted (using a crude expression to describe the insult), "Washington is far away, *mais les engueulades sont proches*" (but its upbraiding is near at hand).

On Friday, June 7, we received our exit permits from France and we were ready to board the *SS Washington*, docked at Le Verdon on the Gironde estuary. It was scheduled to depart on Saturday, June 8, the last American ship to leave war-torn France. The good-bye was heartrending, but the last month had been so stressful that I felt numb. Everything happened so quickly that my memory is somewhat blurred. I can only recall boarding the train at the railway station in Bordeaux and finding ourselves in a compartment with an elderly Belgian couple whose daughter had married an American after the First World War and worked as a secretary to Roosevelt: she had had no difficulty securing visas for her parents.

We left the French coast at about eight o'clock in the evening of June 8, and I recall standing on deck with my sister, quite shaken at the thought that I was leaving the European coast, not knowing whether or when I would see it again. To my shock and amazement, just as the *Washington* was pulling away from the dock, my sister, who, again, knew my aunt and uncle much better than me, turned to me and said, "Life will not always be easy." I understood that she was referring to *my* life, but I did not fully grasp her meaning, so I asked her, "Why didn't you warn me?" She answered simply that it would be an "interesting adventure." Her words turned out to be prophetic: life for me would be a great struggle. We would not see our parents again until June of 1946 after a separation of six years, and during this period, my life would take a totally unexpected turn.

The first leg of the trip was arduous. We crossed the Bay of Biscay, well known for its rough waters, and both my sister and I became dreadfully seasick. My sister had suffered from carsickness since she was a child, but I had convinced myself that I could control the situation using "mind over matter," which certainly was not the case. I had hoped to take care of my sister, whom I loved dearly, but in fact I was as miserable as she.

Early Monday morning we arrived in Lisbon where I was gratefully enriched by a distinctively southern landscape. We were not permitted to dock, but American citizens, escaping from war-torn Europe, were brought onto the *Washington* all day long. The ship's usual capacity was close to a thousand passengers, but because of the emergency, the large ball room, tennis courts, and library had been transformed into dormitories to accommodate the two-thousand who were expected by the time the *Washington* would pick up a last contingent from Galway, Ireland. My sister and I traveled first class, but because of the situation, two cots had been added to the room and we were joined on the journey by two Russian women. We left the Portuguese capital during the night.

Now comes the episode with which I began my story, namely our close encounter with the Nazi U-boat and the unforgettable experience in which my entire life had suddenly flashed before me. There I was, standing arm-in-arm with my sister, Louloute, looking out into the misty ocean. I was convinced I would die. Strangely, I cannot say I was frightened. I was ready, or rather, I was numb. Had I found myself in the same situation later in life, I think I would have clung more resolutely to life. Over time, one's roots grow stronger.

Gradually, we learned that the captain seemed to be sending signals to the Nazi U-boat, and after a couple of anguishing hours we were told that the danger had passed. The all-clear signal was given, and the crew labored to restart the engines so that we might proceed north to Ireland. We anchored in Galway harbor without docking. We remained until all the passengers fleeing England and Ireland had been brought aboard. June 14 is one of the longest days of the year, and I recall still being able to read on deck at ten-thirty in the evening. On Friday, June 21, we finally arrived in New York where my uncle, who was waiting for us, managed to board the ship to greet us. While on the trading floor on Wall Street, he had seen the announcement that the Washington had been intercepted by a German U-boat. By then, we were probably already on our way, but for hours he lived in fear of the worst consequences. He was visibly moved by the thought that two of his brother-in-law's daughters might have perished at sea.

CHAPTER 3

The scene of my life now shifts to New York City. But let me complete—by way of a dramatic interlude—the tale of my father, Henri, and his siblings, particularly his brothers Léon and Fr. Robert, during the years 1940–1942. Whatever they received in common through their shared upbringing, it is difficult to imagine more divergent paths. My family was marked both by tragedy and greatness.

Two other siblings played a minor role in the drama inasmuch as they were not in Belgium. A member of the Belgian army, my uncle Pierre was arrested at the time of the German invasion and spent four years, until 1944, in a German prison camp. My aunt Laure had emigrated to New York with her husband, Robert Brunner, and was living at the Waldorf Astoria. It was to stay with my aunt and uncle that my sister, Louloute and I were traveling to America.

I already alluded to Léon and his wife Claire as having been German sympathizers during World War I. Alas, those sympathies degenerated into outspoken support for the Nazis. "Hitler will save us from Communism," they said. Their son and my first cousin, Étienne, who was exactly my age, volunteered for the Belgian contingent in the German SS Waffen under the command of the Belgian traitor, Léon Degrelle. Fairly soon after, in 1942, he was killed wearing the Nazi uniform on the Russian front.

After Louloute and I had boarded the SS Washington, my parents did not remain long in the awful apartment where we had stayed in Bordeaux. They left for Arcachon, a lovely town on the Atlantic coast, until they could safely go back to Belgium. It would have been slow going given the disruptions of war.

Fr. Robert, who had already parted ways with my family in Moulins, managed to go to England in a small boat, where he served as chaplain to the French and Belgian soldiers in exile. Nearly two years later, in 1942, he volunteered to undertake a most dangerous mission, even though he was over forty-five. He was parachuted into southern Belgium by the Allies to gather crucial information. He was supposed to jump with another man whose task was to bury the parachutes and the only one carrying a spade. When the time came, his companion panicked. "Fr. Jourdain, I am taken by such fears," he said, "please jump first." My uncle jumped, but the other man never followed. Only weeks later did he learn that the man had jumped so poorly that he got caught in the wheels of the plane. A tragic end. After waiting in vain, my uncle tried his best to hide the parachute by digging with his hands, but, of course, without the spade, he could not do the job properly. Later it was discovered by the Nazis who then knew that a spy had landed.

My uncle managed to see all the key people in Belgium. He also met with my father, who knew that to see his beloved brother, whose cover at any moment could be compromised, could mean torture and death. The three brothers, Henri, Fr. Robert, and Léon, were within a few miles of each other—and just at a moment when their political and moral commitments had all but severed their family bonds.

Through the fantastic organization of the British intelligence, Fr. Robert managed to leave Belgium and go all through France in small stages. By the time he arrived at the border of Spain, the Nazis, who had feverishly been working to discover the identity of the spy, found out who he was and alerted the Franco government (which was allied with Hitler, though the Nazis were not permitted on Spanish soil). He was arrested and held at the concentration camp in Miranda de Ebro. It is hard to imagine that the Nazis did not ask the Spanish to turn him over to them, which, to their credit, they did not do. My uncle's liberation remains shrouded in mystery, but he was soon released and brought to Gibraltar, and then flown by private plane back to England. He would receive the highest honors from the British, French, and Belgian governments. He then resumed his work as a chaplain to the French and Belgian contingents in England. Having discovered Fr. Robert's identity, it was not long before the Nazis had assembled a list of all the people he had seen. This included my father, who was arrested and interrogated for eight hours. My father was not an intellectual, but he had a quick Latin mind and managed to escape all the traps they set for him, responding so cleverly and without contradicting himself that he betrayed no one, which greatly frustrated his interrogators. They got nowhere. Speaking German to one another, one of them suddenly realized that my father understood their every word. "Sprechen sie Deutsch?" the German soldier shouted. "Selbstverständlich" (of course)! my father answered. He and his siblings had had a Ger-

man Fräulein for their governess and until he was a teenager all the children spoke German. My father's German
was strongly flavored by a Cologne accent as his governess
had come from the Rhineland. This seemed to impress the
Nazis. They let him go, which was nothing short of a miracle. He had not heard or spoken a single word of German
for twenty-four years—not since World War I when the
Germans had occupied Belgium for four years. Following
World War I, Belgium hatred for Germany was so intense
that if someone spoke a word of that despised language,
people would practically spit in their face.

Everyone else my uncle, Fr. Robert, had visited was
caught and sent to concentration camps. Not a single person came back alive. Only my father was spared this fate.
My youngest sister, Titane, was not yet seven at the time.
My mother showed an admirable courage throughout this
fearful trial.

In late 1944 (or possibly early 1945), Fr. Robert once
again parachuted into Holland where he joined the Belgian
troops. When the war ended in May 1945, he went back
to his Jesuit life in Belgium. His superiors knew they had
a hero among them, but typical of authentic Jesuit spirituality they did not allow him to give public talks about his
activities. On the contrary, to preserve his humility, they
appointed him to a modest position at the Jesuit college
in Liège, where he spent the last ten years of his life. It was
only after his death that his heroism was recognized.

My mother, of course, knew nothing. Was my father
part of a "chain" providing information through my uncle?
Where did they meet? How often? I do not know. My
father was a tomb.

After the war, my beloved father received some sort of honor for his heroism. My mother found out quite accidentally when, one day, a lady congratulated her husband's bravery during the war. My mother did not know what she was alluding to. "Don't you know that your husband was honored?" the lady asked. Apparently it was in the newspapers. My mother then asked my father, "Did you get an award?" "Yes." "What did you with it?" "After reading it, I tore it up and put it in the wastepaper basket."

After his death my mother opened his mail. There were many letters from missions and religious organizations describing him as one of their most generous benefactors and asking about his whereabouts. My mother had never suspected how much of his earnings he gave to the Church. That was Henri Jourdain.

To think that the five children of Louis and Alice Jourdain could find themselves in such vastly different situations. Pierre: locked in a German prison camp. Laure: residing in splendor at the Waldorf in New York. My father, Henri: in Brussels with my mother and younger sisters. Fr. Robert: a priest, patriot, and quiet hero. And Léon . . . alas, Léon. I almost do not dare to raise the nightmare question: what would Léon have done had he known of Fr. Robert's secret mission on behalf of the Allies or of his meeting with my father?

But God is merciful. He is the father of the prodigal son, he is the good shepherd. I pray for each of the deceased members of my family. May they have found mercy. May they rest in peace.

CHAPTER 4

Louloute and I had arrived in New York. Having been retrieved by our uncle Robert Brunner, his chauffeur took us to the Waldorf Astoria where my aunt awaited our arrival. The following months would be some of the most trying of my life. Unlike my sister Louloute, I was associated with the van de Vorsts (my mother's side) and thus with the "wrong" side of the family. Why? Like my mother's brothers (especially two of the four), who were like fireworks, I had a quick wit and talent for fast replies. Not surprisingly the van de Vorsts were lawyers who could tend toward the flamboyant, while the Jourdains, serious and factual, were engineers. Louloute was "free" to do as she pleased, while I was made to serve as an assistant to my uncle's secretary, standing for hours on end in a closet, putting files in order. I ardently desired to pursue my studies, but was made to understand that I was not up to the task. In 1941, I was even sent to a secretarial school, the Wood School on 42nd Street, to render me a bit more efficient. Needless to say, I was neither asked nor consulted.

In order to accommodate our arrival, my aunt and uncle had arranged for a larger apartment, and so, the following fall, we moved to the 39th floor of the Waldorf, a residential portion called the Towers. Our residence had four sunlit exposures: north, south, east, and west.

We lived at the Waldorf for six years, from June 21, 1940 to June 4, 1946, although summers were spent in Stockbridge, Massachusetts located in the beautiful Berkshire region. We always stayed at Heaton Hall, an old-fashioned hotel, which, I am told, has since burned down. (The property now belongs to the Marians of the Immaculate Conception whose American headquarters are in Stockbridge.) Counting the months, we spent maybe a total of a year in this lovely, small New England town.

Despite the trying experience of being, from day one, a "second-class" member of the family, and despite feeling hopelessly lost and uprooted, I did experience moments of great solace. Whenever I entered St. Patrick's Cathedral and heard the words, "*Introibo ad altare Dei . . .*" ("I shall go in to the altar of God"), I felt completely "at home" and I understood that I would always be fully "at home" on earth wherever the Holy Catholic Church uttered these sacred words. The Mass was the very same, in every single detail, as the one I had heard in my home country since I was four years old. Here were my roots. To this day, these words, used for centuries and centuries, touch my heart— for in them I can taste the golden cord of tradition.

The two and a half years between June 21, 1940 and November 27, 1942 were the most somber of my entire life. My uncle succeeded in making me feel that he would have much preferred if my sister Louloute had come alone. Whether we took a walk, whether his chauffeur drove to see the surroundings of New York (the beautiful drive along the Hudson) or whether we went to a restaurant, I always felt what the French call "*de trop,*" meaning "superfluous."

But had I refused to accompany them, I would have been accused of being in a bad mood. It was a no-win situation.

My aunt, convinced that she had to correct the mistakes that her sister-in-law had made in our education (particularly mine, with a van de Vorst temperament) played the pedagogue, and probably with the best will, made every possible pedagogical mistake one could imagine. Even though I was in my late teens, I could not make any decisions of my own: at first she chose our clothing, our hats, and our daily occupations. That I was sent to a secretarial school—the last thing I, who had a very clear intellectual interest, would have chosen—was obviously imposed on me with a definite purpose. She thought that the van de Vorsts were much too self-assured, and on the other hand she hinted at the fact that I was not particularly talented and therefore unable to study in a foreign language.

What can a teenager do in a foreign country, with a very primitive knowledge of the language (we went to the Berlitz School at Rockefeller Center twice a week), but swallow the pill and keep silent? But inside I was deeply unhappy. Thank God, I had my faith, and went daily to St. Patrick's for Mass. But I was in a dark tunnel.

My uncle was a finance man. He had no intellectual interests besides contemporary history (he read biographies of famous personalities). But he was not spiritually formed. My aunt, by contrast, was a very talented woman: well-read in religion, philosophy, and literature. She was definitely intelligent, though too convinced of her wisdom and pedagogical talents.

I never spoke to anyone about my problems, least of all

to my aunt's confessor, Fr. Hebrant, a Jesuit who escaped from Belgium with us who was residing at Fordham, and who was also the confessor of Empress Zita, who lived in a convent on 14th Street.

In grammar school, I developed a bad case of hepatitis. I was very sick (which happened frequently when I was a child) and the result was that my liver was very sensitive. Body and soul are a mysterious unity, and no doubt my psychological misery triggered a renewed attack of hepatitis.

As my condition worsened, I saw a Jewish physician named Dr. Violin whose office, I recall, was between Madison and Park on 87th Street, very close to the Church of St. Ignatius. He had come to us at the Waldorf several times and, being very perceptive, he immediately "felt" the atmosphere and sensed that my situation was not an easy one. He ordered tests, and as expected, my liver was badly swollen. He called me to his office, told me about my condition, recommended some pills, and then out of a blue sky, said to me, "I think you should see a psychiatrist." I jumped out of my seat. I did not know much about Freud, but enough to be very suspicious, and "smelled" that he was influenced by this fashionable "genius" who was taking America by storm at the time.

"Are you out of your mind?" I exclaimed. "Yes, my situation is very difficult, but the only solution is to deepen my spiritual life." He was clearly taken by surprise, but kept silent.

In 1942, I was finally permitted to resume my beloved studies, first on a part-time basis and then, in 1943, as a full-time student. Since I had completed high school, and possibly two years of college before leaving Belgium, I was far enough ahead of the other students that I still managed to receive my BA from Manhattanville in May, 1944.

Despite being permitted to take courses, my aunt believed I was not talented enough to get a degree. She suggested that my father would be ruined after the war and given that not all girls get married, I would have to earn a living. Because of my love for books, she concluded that my calling in life was to become a librarian. Needless to say, I was not consulted. Even though my courses were fully paid for, she told the superior that I was to work six hours a week in the library, to get the training needed. My fellow workers were all students on scholarship who had to earn money to pay for their studies.

So in September 1942, I entered the library and the head librarian had me move books from one side of the library to the other. They were put on a trolley, and then placed on a shelf. Not only was this work boring, I truly did not see how it would give me the training I needed to become a librarian.

One day, the trolley was particularly full, and while pushing it a book fell off the shelf. I picked it up. It was In Defense of Purity by Dietrich von Hildebrand. The title attracted me, and I opened the book and starting reading. Seeing me, the librarian, who was the incarnation of efficiency, came over to express her displeasure, "you are here to work, not to read." I obeyed, and continued transporting books until the hour was over. Two weeks later I would meet Dietrich von Hildebrand in person.

CHAPTER 5

One of my professors at Manhattanville was a German refugee by the name of Balduin Schwarz. It was through him that I made the acquaintance of his own teacher and friend, Dietrich von Hildebrand, who was then professor at Fordham University. Professor Schwarz told me that von Hildebrand would be giving a talk in his apartment at 448 Central Park West, and that I would be heartily welcome to attend. Attractive as this was, I was convinced that my aunt and uncle would never allow me to attend. Imagine my surprise when they gave me their permission. On Friday, November 27, 1942, I walked toward Sixth Avenue to take the subway to Columbus Circle, and then the local to 103rd Street.

Together with another Belgian student, I walked the final few blocks to the shabby building where the von Hildebrands lived. After ringing the bell at 5F, we entered the very modest lobby. What a contrast to the splendor of the Waldorf.

Professor Schwarz had told us that his friend had just recovered from a very severe case of pneumonia, and asked us to leave right after the talk. We rang the bell and I heard steps moving toward us quickly. The door swung open, and there was Dietrich von Hildebrand who greeted us so warmly that I was overwhelmed by his spontaneous kindness. What a contrast with the icy and formal atmosphere of the Waldorf.

I then had a very strange experience: somehow I had the feeling that I had met him before. I knew that he had escaped from France, and later that evening on my way back to the Waldorf, I tried to relive the days I spent in that country between May 15 and June 8. Where could I possibly have seen him? Later when he told me about his escape through France at the very same time, I realized that we could not possibly have met. Much later, I read in Kierkegaard what he felt upon meeting Regina Olson, "Oh! Can I really believe the report of the poets that when one sees for the first time the beloved object he believes that he has seen her long before, that all love like all knowledge is recollection?"

The apartment was very modest. One entered directly into a corridor. On the left there was a very modest bedroom facing a narrow, dark courtyard, while two larger rooms faced Central Park West. He soon started his talk: the topic was "transformation in Christ," the title of his great book. His topic was "the readiness to change," which is also the title of the first chapter of the book. From the first moment he began to speak, I felt that he was feeding my soul with a food I had always longed for. He spoke out of a deep spirit of recollection, and I drank in every word.

He had holes in his shoes, and I could see that he was living in great poverty. At the time, I had no idea what a contrast this formed with his upbringing in one of the great artistic families of Germany. He must have spoken for some fifty minutes, and then heeding the words of Professor Schwarz not to dally after the talk, we thanked him warmly and took our leave.

After twenty-nine months of darkness, the sun again rose in my life. As I traveled back to the Waldorf, I experienced a joy I had not tasted since my arrival in New York. But it was more than a revival of a past happiness. He also opened something new to me, a new joy and freshness in the life of faith which, despite my deeply religious upbringing, I had never encountered before. I had grown wings, and said to myself: this is what I was longing to hear.

My experience was not unique. As I later learned, many others were similarly affected by their first encounter with von Hildebrand. I wholeheartedly concur with what Professor Schwarz wrote many years later in a remembrance of his beloved teacher, "I had never in my life met someone so happy. I did not realize it was possible to be so happy." But this was not just the happiness of a cheerful soul; it was the joy of a living faith in which he consciously lived from moment to moment. I cannot count how many people were drawn to faith because of his joy.

I was so impressed by the content of von Hildebrand's talk that I decided to learn German so that I could have access to the book which would have such a great influence on my life. I acquired a Gospel in German, I think a copy lent to me by von Hildebrand. I made rapid progress because German is so similar in grammar and vocabulary to the Flemish (a Dutch dialect) I had studied for twelve years since grammar school in Belgium.

Still a junior, Manhattanville allowed me to begin taking courses with Dietrich von Hildebrand at Fordham in 1943. Having earned my BA in 1944, I immediately entered Fordham where I received my MA in philosophy in 1946. I had by then most of the credits needed for a PhD in philosophy, which I wanted to complete at Fordham.

My uncle and aunt, however, had other plans: after the war ended in 1945, they decided they wanted us to return to Belgium. They were accustomed to making decisions that were obeyed without being challenged. So it was that despite my blossoming academic aspirations in New York and my hopes of completing my studies at Fordham, June 1946 found my sister and me on a flight to Brussels by way of Newfoundland, Ireland, and finally, Amsterdam, where we stayed overnight. Six years earlier, we had left with an inkling of the horror that was descending upon Europe. Now we saw the havoc and destruction that had taken place. Despite the relatively short distance between Amsterdam and Brussels (just over 100 miles), our train ride the next day across the war-torn countryside to the Belgian capital consumed an entire day. We arrived at seven in the evening to find our beloved father waiting on the platform to receive us.

My parents also wished me to stay home, but I was eager to finish my studies in the US. Over their objections, and the opposition of my aunt and uncle, they finally relented and allowed me to return to the US. Traveling was so difficult at the time (October, 1946), that I had to take a cargo ship across the Atlantic in a trip that took nineteen days and included terrible storms. By November 1, I was back in New York City, sharing a shabby apartment with a friend, Madeleine Froelicher (whose friendship is one of the greatest gifts of my life), all in striking contrast to the luxurious Waldorf apartment where I had lived with my aunt and uncle.

My father had given me a modest sum of money that enabled me to complete my coursework, but by the fall of 1947, it had dwindled to practically nothing and I decided to apply for a teaching job. I sent my Curriculum vitae to Catholic colleges in and around New York. I was a good student, and felt confident I would soon find a position.

I was mistaken, however, and received one refusal after another. "It is not the policy of Catholic colleges to appoint women to teach philosophy," I was told. Let us not forget that St. Edith Stein, with a PhD summa cum laude, had to earn her living teaching Latin in a Catholic high school. And I was no Edith Stein!

I began to seriously worry. What was I going to do? One day, I went to confession to Fr. John Oesterreicher (whom I had met through Dietrich von Hildebrand—they had closely collaborated in Vienna in their fight against anti-Semitism), and who at the time was assistant pastor at a parish on West 49th Street. I had given him my Masters' thesis on Uti and Frui in the Philosophy of Saint Augustine to read, and he had liked it.

After confession, we chatted on the steps of the church. I told him that I was desperately looking for a teaching job but had been turned down by all the Catholic colleges to which I had applied. He replied that just a few days before he had made the acquaintance of Professor James O'Gorman, chairman of the Department of Psychology and Philosophy at Hunter College, one of the four colleges within the City University of New York. "I'll write him a letter of recommendation. Why don't you try your luck there?" I was less than thrilled at the prospect: to teach at a secular university would never have crossed my mind.

True to his word, Fr. Oesterreicher sent a letter to Professor O'Gorman. The letter happened to arrive the very day one of Hunter's philosophy professors, Dr. Emmanuel Chapman, took a leave of absence; he had been diagnosed with cancer and needed an urgent operation.

That was on Friday, December 5. The chairman to whom Fr. Oesterreicher had written called me and asked if I would be willing to take a substitute position beginning the following Monday, from December 8 until December 23. I was to teach at Hunter downtown. I was briefly interviewed by Professor McGill of the Philosophy department, and was formally offered the job. I had to accept.

The weekend was nightmarish. I worked with the kind of intensity that only despair can fuel. I felt terribly insecure. I had never taught in my life. Moreover, with my European background which presumed respectful, receptive students, I knew I was ill-equipped to face assertive (and often arrogant) students who came from a totally secular background.

I prayed.

I was given a fifteen-hour schedule which spanned Monday to Friday, nine to twelve. I vividly recall the trepidation with which I entered the classroom assigned to me on the 7th floor, facing noisy Park Avenue. I imagine that my teaching was as bad as any other tyro and when I left the building at noon, I had the feeling I had been a total failure. I fully expected to receive a pink slip the very next day.

But Professor O'Gorman astonished me by informing me that the students were pleased with my performance, and so I persevered until the Christmas break. I had taught thirty hours, and my total pay was some $80 dollars (minus taxes). This was the first money I had ever earned, and I was grateful.

Dr. Chapman returned in January, but to my pleasant surprise, the chairman offered me a full load of fifteen hours teaching for the new veterans program in the Bronx, which Hunter was opening to offer a free education to the GIs returning from Europe and Asia. A new staff was needed immediately, and the position fell into my grateful hands. (At that time, Hunter and what is now Lehman College were one institution, with Hunter downtown operating as an all-female college.)

The salary was a bit better, paying $225 for each course and, as I lived frugally, I could cover my daily expenses. I accepted.

However, my acceptance was mingled with great trepidation. All of a sudden, I—a young woman, aged twenty-four—was to face an older, all-male student body, most from poor or disadvantaged backgrounds. I had the feeling that these men were not exactly raised to be perfect gentlemen. I was grateful for the opportunity but also petrified.

So, in late January 1948, I took the subway to the Kingsbridge Station in the Bronx and walked another ten minutes to what was called at the time, Hunter uptown. The campus was extraordinarily unattractive with only a few neglected buildings located on a huge, steeply sloped tract of land. My fears proved to be fully justified. I had five sections, all-in-all one-hundred and fifty students, all pleased to receive a free education as former GIs, but most of whom could not have cared less about philosophy. The

BA was a pure means to getting a job. As expected, they entered my classroom strongly influenced by the relativism they had imbibed already in their high school education. As they began to realize that I would be challenging their views, they "woke up" and voiced their opposition. It was always the same refrain: to claim that truth is objective is to introduce the germs of totalitarianism. Each man has the right to choose his own truth. I often held my hands under my desk, for fear that my students would see them trembling. It was terribly demanding, but I carried on all the same, even though I felt that I was a total failure.

Despite moments of discouragement with the GIs, and the fear that I was achieving nothing, imagine my joy when I gave final examinations around the middle of June 1948 and found a note in one of the tests. The student had written, "When I entered your classroom, I had kicked out religion. Now I shall go back to Church."

I was amazed, for I had never mentioned religion in my courses. But I should not have been surprised. Throughout my career, I found that the greatest obstacle to faith was always some form of relativism. Once removed, those who "have good will" always find their way to God. I was overwhelmed with joy. After all, my "blood, sweat and tears" had not been in vain.

Had this student only known how much these hasty words, scribbled on a dirty piece of paper, meant to me! Professors were given only forty-eight hours to correct tests and I had one-hundred and fifty exams to grade. The work was feverish, from morning to night, but I was willing to accept such suffering if only I could be instrumental in helping a single soul find God. Man longs for truth and sometimes it takes only a word to rekindle this longing.

I believe my students knew intuitively that I never tried to foist my "opinions" upon them to win them over to a particular camp, but that I considered the knowledge of truth to be a treasure which I wished with all my heart to share. Truth is never the possession of the one who sees it. Truth is always "ours."

CHAPTER 6

The note announcing my student's return to the Church was the first of many points of light that would illuminate a career in which I experienced much darkness. Yet right from the start, I was also privileged to witness the drama which is every person's pursuit of ultimate questions. How can I ever forget an encounter I had with a student in the fall semester shortly before Christmas 1948? He seemed to have a real interest in the course. He raised intelligent questions and after class would wait for me at the exit and accompany me to the subway, a good ten-minute walk in a part of the Bronx that was not very safe. It was winter and often pitch-black.

At the end of the semester, I raised the question of God's existence—a daring thing to do. All of a sudden, this same student was up-in-arms. He challenged, he objected, he tried to ridicule my arguments. I was happy when the hour was over. I assumed he would not wait for me, but I was mistaken. There he was at the exit. It was a clear, crisp, cold winter night. The moon was bright, the stars shining and the sky dark blue on this night. We both looked up admiring this beauty. To break the silence, I said, "Look at this magnificence!" All of a sudden he raised his fist and shouted, "He was capable of creating the moon, and I cannot." His expression was one of rage and hatred. Very quietly I said, "That explains your opposition in the classroom."

This incident taught me a great deal. I realized that much of my students' opposition stemmed not from intellectual difficulties but from pride or from fear that their way of life might be challenged. Although their counter arguments were clothed in intellectual garments, they were really a kind of cover-up. One can understand why a student might not forgive a professor who succeeds in awakening their conscience, especially if the student now experiences guilt. Kierkegaard is right. Speaking of religious and ethical truths, he writes, "All men are more or less afraid of the truth."*

Nietzsche wrote, "My will said to my intellect: this cannot be, and my intellect gave in." Truths that are "neutral" and do not affect one's life are easily accepted, because "who cares?" It would be strange indeed if a person had a nervous breakdown upon finding out that the sum of the angles of a triangle are equal to two right angles. It is different with religious, metaphysical, or ethical truths. I recall that a few years later, one of my students said to me in front of the whole class, "The worst thing that could happen to me would be to find out that I have an immortal soul; then my actions would have consequences for me." It was a tragically honest insight.

There were a great many Jewish students at the city university. I met Orthodox Jews (who were often among my very best students), Conservative, Reformed, Hasidic Jews (as visitors in my classroom), and alas, some atheist Jews. In many respects, my Jewish students were among

---

* The Journals of Kierkegaard, translated by Alexander Dru (Harper Torchbooks), p. 202.

the most gifted and receptive I would have. But I can recall often being gravely disappointed that some members of the Jewish community at Hunter did not share a commitment to the objectivity of truth. I recall that I shared an office with a Jewish professor, and one day a Jewish student came to him and asked him about God. The answer was categorical, "Each man is entitled to choose his own god: for some it is thunder, for others an animal, for another a statue." For the first time in my life, I realized that some of the chosen people had totally abandoned their sacred tradition. I had naively assumed that to be Jewish meant to be a believer. Alas, I discovered that I was mistaken; it grieved me profoundly. For the first (and not the last) time in my career, I found out that many Jews who are "proud" of the privilege of being God's chosen people were simultaneously radical "liberals" and even atheists.

I recall a Jewish student dragging his feet into my classroom, looking very despondent. I said to him, "you do not seem to enjoy the course." His answer was clear and prompt, "Why should your ideas be better than mine? We are all equal." I remarked that the value of an idea depended upon whether it echoed truth, but that struck him as meaningless.

In that same fall semester of 1948, I remember a big, fat fellow who was taking my course on ethics in the Bronx building. It was always a very lively class. At one point, he posed the following question, "What should you do if the alternative were either to kill an innocent person or to be killed?" I could sense that the question most likely engaged him because of his experiences during the war. There was a great deal of agitation in the classroom, with some students speaking out of turn and contradicting one another. I turned back to the student who had set off the controversy: "You have raised the question. What would you do?"

I can still see him in front of me. He had slouched in his chair and, with his hands on his belly, he answered, "That is not much of a problem for me. I have only one life, and I do not want to lose it. I would not hesitate to kill you to save my life." That was a clear position. Some students endorsed it; others called him a coward. My students have never complained that my classes were boring, and here was a case in point. The fat student turned to me at last and said, "So, Dr. Jourdain, if you were in that situation, what would you do?"

I was on the spot. Indeed, what would I do? Had I said, "Of course, I would let myself be killed," I might be expressing some very grave illusions about myself. Had I said, "I would kill you," my whole course on ethics was in jeopardy.

All of a sudden, the answer came to me from above. Sometime before, I had read a beautiful story in Martin Buber, about a rabbi in search of a truly honest man. I told the story to my class.

One day, the rabbi meets a man on the road and asks him, "If you found a bag full of gold, what would you do?" The man answered without hesitation, "Rabbi, I would keep it, praising my good luck." The rabbi looked at him sadly and said, "You are a thief." He posed the question to another who answered, "Rabbi, I would immediately look for the owner and give him back the money." Sadly, the rabbi said, "You are a liar." Then he turned to a third man who, at the thought of having so much gold, got very excited but said, "Rabbi, I would beg God to give me the strength to give it back to its owner." The rabbi said, "You are the man I was looking for."

At that very moment, the bell rang. And I left the classroom. It was perfect timing.

As is to be expected, my students entered my classroom with definite positions on the crucial questions of human existence: God, the immortality of the soul, the meaning of life, moral good and evil. This is something that a philosophy teacher should not lose sight of. How easy by comparison to teach a foreign language to beginners, because students know that they do not know. But every man, because he is a person, is bound to raise questions which—to paraphrase the French philosopher, Jacques Chevalier—every man raises when he faces death.

CHAPTER 7

My first experience of teaching had stretched me enormously. I felt incredibly inadequate and unprepared. But the challenge so far had come from my students. Now I was to get my first taste of academic politics. Louise Cowan, one of the founders of the University of Dallas, apparently said, "I never knew the meaning of evil until I served on a faculty committee." She was not exaggerating.

Dr. Chapman, whom I had replaced prior to taking my new position in the Bronx, returned to Hunter. Already in April, he had to acknowledge defeat: in spite of his courageous fight, he was a dying man. Once again, a substitute was urgently needed. My chair said he would gladly have taken me, but I was teaching full-time in the Bronx, another substitute had to be found, and so Dr. Henry Rosenthal was chosen. However, the chairman, Dr. O'Gorman, said that a tenure track position would open, and that he would be glad to appoint me when the time came.

So, when Dr. Chapman died, I would, under normal circumstances, have applied for the position. However, as "luck" would have it, my friend and former professor from Manhattanville, Balduin Schwarz, applied for the job. He knew Dr. George Shuster, the president of Hunter College, and the latter had told him, "You have the job in your pocket." There seemed no point in applying for the vacant position: Dr. Schwarz was infinitely better qualified than I.

It was then that I made my first acquaintance with Hunter politics. The Personnel and Budget Committee (the committee that appoints teachers and recommends tenures and promotions) was called to vote on his appointment, and it appeared that his chances were good: he had taught for quite a few years, had written a couple of excellent books, had authored articles, and knew several languages.

However, a member of the committee told me "confidentially" that just as the faculty was about to vote, the chairman had received a call from the president, George Shuster, saying that he wanted Dr. Rosenthal to be appointed instead (breaking his promise to Dr. Schwarz). The whole thing was, of course, political, and rumored to be atonement for a few articles Shuster had published in *Commonweal* magazine back in the thirties, praising National Socialism. Quite understandably, this pitiful lack of judgment on his part had antagonized the Jewish faculty. Shuster was of German descent and had been impressed for a while by Hitler's promise to reestablish the greatness of Germany, which had been so deeply humiliated by its defeat in 1918. His eyes were later opened, but nevertheless, his praise of Hitler had left a black mark on his record, his reputation with Jewish professors tarnished. He had some "repair work" to do, and he did it very cleverly until he retired.[*]

I was shocked and disappointed. Not only had the president broken his word, but the appointee clearly lacked the

---

[*] Shuster was later appointed to serve as assistant to Fr. Theodore Hesburgh, president of Notre Dame. He remained at Notre Dame until his death in 1977.

qualifications of Professor Schwarz. Rosenthal had a PhD in philosophy, it is true, but as far as I knew he had never taught (or at most, very little) and had headed Hillel at Hunter (the Jewish campus organization), a job which he had then lost. Experiences like these taught me how little concern was shown to what was best for the students, or for the "democratic" process. It was a sad lesson: in academia, politics dominates.

I took my comprehensive examinations for the PhD in the spring of 1948: three six-hour written exams administered on a series of consecutive Saturdays. I passed the exams and began to turn my thoughts to the dissertation, which would be difficult to write while teaching full-time.

In the summer of 1948, I went to Europe to visit my family and do some research-work for my dissertation. In the spring of 1949, my teaching load happened to be reduced to eleven hours. Financially, this was bad news, but it was also providential, as there was one less class to prepare and fewer exams to correct. I could devote more time to my dissertation.

Since discovering philosophy in 1942 and reading St. Augustine's *Confessions*, I had had a great love and awe for this gigantic Catholic thinker. What he wrote was not only luminously true and brilliantly formulated, but enriching for my intellectual, spiritual, and religious life. How profoundly this great saint understood the mystery of the human soul, its contradictions, its greatness, and its weaknesses. I had devoted my MA thesis to him and decided to expand my knowledge by writing my PhD dissertation on him as well.

My decision to write on St. Augustine would later prove a most infelicitous choice. The very word "saint" was unacceptable in the philosophy department of a radically secular college. It was—and would remain—a black mark on my Curriculum vitae. My theme was The Role of Created Goods in the Philosophy of Saint Augustine. The following fifteen months were incredibly strenuous: preparing courses, correcting term papers and exams, and doing the research work on my dissertation, which I began to write.

It was so demanding that it took all my time and dedication. I do not think I ever had a day off. I worked feverishly to present my thesis in May 1949 and received my PhD in June. I had just turned twenty-six. One heavy burden was taken off my shoulders. At times, I wondered why I, whose youth had been so protected, had chosen to lead such an exhausting life.

During this stressful time, my beloved father suffered a severe heart attack, a common form of death in his family. Of course, he was at home in Belgium, while I was in New York. He was unconscious for several days, and it was really quite miraculous that he recovered. As a very pious man and a daily communicant, being unable to receive Holy Communion during his acute illness was a severe trial for him.

I endured weeks of deep anxiety, concerned about my father (who, though he did recover, aged quite a bit), and concerned about my family at home, as my youngest sister was not yet fourteen.

∾

At that time, the Hunter philosophy department, because of its very small size, was housed in the Psychology Department, and it remained that way until 1962. The faculty included a professor by the name of Jerauld McGill, who enjoyed a certain reputation because he had published quite a bit. He was a typical intellectual Communist, totally absorbed in "ideas" to create a paradisiacal world. Unwittingly, he must have done great harm. He was impressed because my classes were always full and I heard that he once commented that I was the best-read person in the department. (Hardly a compliment, given that the general level was not impressive.) His remark probably did more harm than good (as did certain high praise given me by O'Gorman) which only enraged my colleagues.

A second, James Gordon Clapp, was a liberal, and, I fear, a non-practicing Catholic; he had written his PhD dissertation on Locke. Another was Gertrude Delahunt, a Catholic, who was looked down upon because she was considered "unworthy" to teach in the Department of Philosophy. (Her field had been education, and later she received an MA in philosophy, but she had no PhD). She taught mostly introductory courses.

There was the new appointee, Henry Rosenthal, who became the fourth member of the department, and who was a liberal Jew and a great admirer of Hegel. He had earned a PhD in philosophy many years before, and, as I already mentioned, worked as director of Hillel at Hunter until losing that position, and was then appointed to the philosophy department by Shuster.

Finally, there was John Somerville, a Communist, who was clever enough to avoid losing his job (as McGill did) when the House Committee on Un-American Activities began to purge universities of some of the most ardent disciples of Karl Marx. Many years later, in 1963, my husband and I were invited to give talks at the University of Rhode

Island. There was a dinner to honor my husband, and I was seated next to the chairman of the philosophy department, a man by the name of Oliver Martin. In the course of conversation he asked me whether I was doing any professional work. I said, yes, that I was teaching philosophy. He asked where, to which I responded, "at Hunter College." He said bluntly, "I don't believe you." "It is a fact," I said. He then asked, "Do you know John Somerville?" "Yes, indeed, he is one of my colleagues," I responded. Professor Martin, who was a Catholic revert, said, "Do you know that in the late 1930s, John Somerville and I were paid by the Communist Party—and well paid—to spread atheism in the academic world? I found my way back to the Church, but Somerville is still a committed Communist."

I recall that one kind colleague in another department advised me to go to "faculty parties." She told me, "It is crucial for your career; this is how the faculty will get to know you; it will increase your chances of receiving a regular appointment." In spite of my exhausting schedule, I did attend one. There was a lot of noise, a lot of smoke, and a lot of drinking. At one point a professor in his late forties turned to me, and said, "I was told that French is your mother tongue. I think it is a beautiful language; would you be willing to teach it to me?" I mumbled that I would be happy to help if I had time. "Do you know the best way of learning a language?" he asked whispering confidentially. "On a pillow!" he said with a guffaw. I was disgusted and did not stay long. I never tried to find out his name. It was the last time I attended one of those parties.

CHAPTER 8

For a while, beginning in 1949 (at which time I was teaching both uptown and downtown) another difficulty arose: a young woman, the pet student of one of my colleagues, was appointed full-time to teach in the day session. Sooner or later, there was bound to be conflict between us—though I hardly ever saw her and we had no contact whatsoever—because we were competitors for the same tenure track, whenever one became available.

I had two objective advantages over her. First, I had just obtained my PhD, while she was still working on hers. Moreover, my classes were always at capacity. She, however, was clever and socially adept, while I struggled daily to remain on my feet, as by this time I was plagued by mononucleosis. It was, of course, most unwise not to socialize. To my amazement, one of my colleagues warned me that my rival was spreading the news that I was anti-Semitic, and advised Jewish students against taking my classes. Though I was rapidly developing a thick skin, I was still shocked to find such rivalry and backbiting among people who are supposed to dedicate their lives to the pursuit of wisdom.

But what could I do? I had been horrified at the Nazi persecution of the Jews and recognized in them a suffering people. But how could I disprove these allegations? What this meant, in practical terms, was that my future at Hunter was very insecure and that my only hope of remaining was to have success in the classroom.

It is very difficult to pass judgment on oneself, but my subjective judgment was that my performance fell far short of what the greatness of the topic called for. But I am sure that my students knew I was totally committed to my teaching, that I loved truth, and that I was not there just to make a living. In the evening session, I was paid by the classroom hour without any medical coverage (which was worrisome because I had a knee problem) and received neither credit nor compensation for time spent counseling students. Nevertheless, I was always ready to give time to needy students, often arriving at Hunter an hour before classes to accommodate them.

In our society a key measure of success is the amount of money one earns. By those standards, I was a failure. My total income for the year 1948, as reported on my IRS return, was $2,413. From the fall semester of 1948 until the fall semester of 1952, I taught both day and evening sessions. One semester, I had five courses; in another, eight; and in still another, seven. Yet my total earnings never exceeded $4,000. But of course, income was never my standard of success. What kept me—and sustained me— were my students.

From day one, there were always a certain number of students for whom what I said offered such a radically new vision that they became devoted followers. Their attachment was not just to my ideas but to me personally.

In 1950, I had such a student, a woman in her late twenties or early thirties who took my course on Introduction to Philosophy. I could see that she was absolutely fascinated. After class she would tell me how beautiful my course was. "You can't imagine what it means to me," she said. "But I'm afraid I'm not truly talented enough really to appreciate what you're giving me. But I'm married to a man who is so incredibly talented, so intelligent. He would understand everything you say. Might I bring him to class?" I agreed. Throughout my career I had many guests in my classroom. One very fine day, there he was. Rarely in my life have I seen a face that oozed so much self-satisfaction. He listened with a sort of paternalistic expression as if to say, "You're doing well, but of course you teach me nothing new." Following the course he thanked me and that was the last I ever saw of him.

The woman had a daughter who was about five years old. One day she approached me to say, "I'm more and more enthusiastic about your class. Would you agree to become the godmother of my daughter?" I said, "But you're not a Catholic." "Yes," came the answer, "but I'd like to become one, even though my husband is a Christian Scientist." I decided to consult the Jesuits on 84th Street. They told me it was possible to accept, despite the prohibition on becoming a godparent of a child whose parents are not Catholic, given the mother's intention to convert. The little girl was baptized at the Church of St. Ignatius in June 1951. (The family lived somewhere nearby on East Side.) I then left for Europe as I did every summer to visit my parents. Upon returning, I bumped into an elderly Catholic woman who taught a few courses in English (having no PhD she was not a member of the faculty). "I've been looking for you," she said, "alas, your godchild died." Apparently a doctor had botched a routine tonsillectomy and accidently severed an artery. "Of course, the mother is in a state of despair and she wants to see you."

Soon after, my former student came to visit me and she was absolutely hysterical with grief. I tried to comfort her as best I could. "The hardest thing is that my husband keeps accusing me of being responsible for her death," she said. As a Christian Scientist, he believed that the events are determined by one's attitude toward them. "He tells me that my pessimism before the operation caused her death," she told me. I did my best to console her. "I can only assume your little girl is with God, infinitely happy and grateful to you for the great gift she had received through you. A newly baptized child of five goes straight to heaven." Two weeks later I again saw the elderly English instructor who gave me the shattering news that my student had gone to Riverside Drive on the Upper West Side and jumped sixteen stories from the rooftop of a building. To this day, I'm convinced that her husband's aim had been to induce her suicide. He was certainly responsible for her death by the way he crushed her with feelings of guilt. I pray for this student of mine whenever I remember her.

CHAPTER 9

I recall an episode in the fall of 1950 which led one of my colleagues to become a lifelong foe. It was a sad affair. The chair of the Psychology Department decided to give the newly appointed Professor Rosenthal the task of making up schedules for the School of General Studies (i.e. evening sessions), which in fact, had already been completed for that semester. I had already been teaching ethics, and the course was so well received that it was filled to capacity.

A special evening session catalogue listed the name of the course and the professor teaching it, and there I was, slated to teach ethics once again. (For some strange reason, at that time, the day session catalogue did not give the name of the professor assigned to give a course. That changed later.) A couple of days before the semester began, however, I received a terse note from Professor Rosenthal, informing me that I was to teach aesthetics and not ethics, even though I was listed for ethics and not aesthetics. I was upset, not only at the tone of the note that gave no explanation or apology, but also because I had prepared to teach ethics and my name was printed in the catalogue. There was no time to prepare the aesthetics class properly. In those days before the computer, evening session teachers were required to spend two days, five hours each day, before each semester, registering students by putting a mark in a box. This task was never given to day session professors. I knew from the registration sheet that, as usual, my course on ethics was filled to capacity, having reached the maximum of forty-five students.

But I had no choice. That first evening, I entered the classroom where aesthetics was scheduled to be taught: it was nearly empty, with at most seven or eight students. The course would be dropped without a minimum of ten, which was a serious matter for someone whose salary depended on each course taught. However, by the second class I found out, to my joy, that enough students had registered to ensure the course was secure.

In the meantime, I learned that Professor Rosenthal had himself taken my course on ethics, for the sake of supplementing his income. He chose Spinoza's ethics as his text book. Naturally, he had chosen a course with a full registration. But when he entered the classroom, (I learned) the students were visibly surprised and upset.

"Isn't Dr. Jourdain teaching this course?" several asked. "No," he replied, "I am." To his consternation, half of the students got up, walked out, went to the registrar, and dropped the course. Compounding this unpleasantness, by his second class, only two students were left of the forty who had originally registered. The course was dropped.

I heard about the affair a few days later, first from a student who had taken a couple of courses with me and was looking forward to a third one, and then from one of the employees in the registrar's office, who told me confidentially about the cancellation of the evening ethics course.

I hoped the whole unpleasant business would be forgotten. Unwittingly, however, I had made a deadly enemy. Of course, I could have had nothing to do with the students' dropping the course: although I knew the number of students who had registered, I did not have access to a roster of names. But Dr. Rosenthal never forgot, and I would pay the price.

But what could I do? It might have been wise to speak to Professor Rosenthal and "apologize," but I thought of the French proverb, "qui s'excuse, s'accuse"—"he who excuses himself accuses himself." Regardless, by the time I came for the evening session at Hunter downtown from the Bronx campus where I spent my days, he and the other day professors had already gone home.

My relationship with another of my colleagues, Professor Clapp, was not much better. Once, in a conciliatory gesture, I asked him if he would care to read an article I had written on Gabriel Marcel. He retorted, "You want me to tear it to pieces?" Another time, I was counseled to win him over by showing appreciation for his work. Obediently, I sat in on one of his classes, where he was expounding Dewey's aesthetics, which is so loaded with errors and so steeped in relativism that I felt like a musician forced to listen to someone singing out-of-tune. He, however, praised the work highly and lectured on the importance of Dewey in our society. After class, I complimented his "scholarly" presentation of the material, but I believe he was intelligent enough to feel that I was not a fan of his.

Another time, we had lunch together in the cafeteria at the Bronx campus. He was going to explain to me how I should teach and correct all the errors I had committed against the university system since 1947. He began by explaining that I had the reputation of teaching Catholicism instead of philosophy. I flatly denied it, as I had not yet understood that to speak of objective truth was already viewed as shoving Catholicism down the students' throats.

Then, the question of God's existence came up. In a city university, one is not supposed to uphold arguments proving God's existence while reserving the right to challenge proofs of His existence. I told the professor that this question was of great interest to the students, and that they always raised it. How could I possibly attack the argument on contingency when I was deeply convinced that it was valid? He responded with the following advice: "What you should do is to expound St. Anselm's proof of God's existence, and then tear it to pieces." Needless to say, that was the last time I asked for advice. I was deeply grieved by his attitude, and discovered how "illiberal" liberal thinkers can be.

As for the charge of teaching religion in the classroom, I found that while professors were given a free hand to "tear to pieces" proofs of God's existence in the name of academic freedom, any discussion of those same proofs, even in an historical context, was condemned as dangerously offensive. Academic freedom was limited to the relativists, subjectivists, and atheists. No "healthy pluralism" here.

In the midst of teaching at Hunter, I had begun devoting all my free time to the writings of Dietrich von Hildebrand. This eminent European philosopher had come to the United States, totally destitute, in December 1940 at the age of fifty-one. He arrived as a refugee, having been one of the most outspoken Catholic voices raised against Hitler and German National Socialism. From the moment I met him, and began reading his works, I was convinced that God had given him an exceptional religious and philosophical mission, and I knew that he was putting these talents at God's service. Like Socrates, he could truthfully say that he was devoting his life to the pursuit of truth. He was a "Knight for Truth."

However, being a rather destitute knight, he could not afford to pay a secretary. He had been writing a book by hand on ethics which was already running into a manuscript of hundreds of pages, but it could not be submitted to a publisher until it was typed. I volunteered to work for him, and in the brief pauses of my mad schedule, managed to type a few pages of this precious manuscript at a time (using the old-fashioned typewriter that I had bought in 1947 to type my PhD dissertation). Whenever he added a page or changed the place of a paragraph, the work had to be done all over again (I believe I typed the manuscript a total of four times). It was overwhelming, but I learned enormously in this labor of love, which was finally published in 1952–1953.

I did not fully realize at the time that this secretarial work through which I inevitably mastered many of his insights was dealing me many of the trump cards I needed to win battles in the classroom. There were certain key ideas of his that served as leitmotivs for all my courses. Of course, I made use of his refutation of empiricism which holds that only empirical evidence can give us certitude. It "cleared the air" to show my students the problematic nature of this view. Though empirical evidence is crucial for the natural sciences, it is woefully inadequate for questions of morality, religion, and aesthetics. Once my students began to see that it was possible to offer evidence of truths that surpassed the empirical level, we could enter deeply into the great questions of philosophy.

The most crucial idea my husband developed was the conceptual-pair "value" and "value-response." Appealing to experience, he wanted to show the difference between things that are good because they bring us pleasure (a warm bath) or even benefit us in some real way (a good meal), and those things that are good in themselves (a moral virtue, a deeply formulated truth, a great work of art). Some responses to values are "adequate," as my husband put it (reverence for virtue or enthusiasm for truth), while others are not (disinterest in beauty or truth).

But the emphasis on truth and value did not mean that complex questions were oversimplified. My students and I spoke of the phenomenon of "value blindness," a concept developed by my husband already in his earliest writings. He wanted to show how, if truth is knowable, so many people, including great thinkers, had derailed into error. To understand value blindness is to recognize the frailty of the human mind, especially its susceptibility to being clouded by pride and disordered human appetites.

Of course, I did not read my husband's books with my students. I simply drew on everything he had given me and which had become second nature through my studies and collaboration with him. Moreover, the insights I had from him, which emerged in the classroom, were formed by my own personality and style. My former students may be better able to explain what enabled me to communicate with such a wide and diverse student body. I certainly did not approach teaching with a plan. I tried to be responsive to each class, always with as much clarity, intensity, wit, and dedication as I could muster.

CHAPTER 10

In 1952, my darling friend Madeleine Froelicher and I decided to take a vacation to Bermuda for a brief respite. My struggle with my mononucleosis was an ongoing battle, but I had to keep this "top secret" and often dragged myself to my classes. Had they known about my daily struggle, they would have seen it as a valid argument for getting rid of me.

Upon returning, I found that there was no work for me in day session and my entire teaching load fell in the evening. From one point of view, this was a blessing. In evening session, I only had to teach four times a week and my commute to and from work was far more manageable. On the other hand, the pay was so low that it was not easy to make ends meet. Evening session was considered to be a kind of "stepchild" and was therefore looked down on. This was a great mistake, because the very best students that I have had were evening session students.

One day in 1953, as I entered the office which Gertrude Delahunt (the only other woman in the department) had kindly allowed me to use when she left in the late morning, I found her waiting for me. Each time the Board of Higher Education had endorsed my modest reappointment, she kindly stayed longer to give me the good news. This time, she seemed to be particularly serious, and told me rather mysteriously that the chairman had just called a meeting of the Personnel and Budget Committee. Usually such meetings were called as an "emergency" so that the voting professors, not knowing the agenda, could not prepare themselves for what was coming.

"There is a tenure track open in philosophy," she told me. I had by then been teaching for about six years at the minimum salary. Tenure meant better hours, medical coverage, a higher salary, and last but not least, the possibility of obtaining tenure after three years, and therefore, job security. "You got the votes, but believe me, it was amazing you made it." But the thunder was just beginning to rumble.

She related the following scenario: the chairman had introduced only one candidate, a young Jewish man who had just received his PhD at Columbia. His name was Michael Wyschogrod. It was clear that he was President Shuster's choice. This is why the meeting was called without warning, and also why his name was the only one on the list of candidates.

However, one member of the committee remarked that voting always implied that several people were proposed and suggested that my name be added to the slate. After all, I had been at Hunter close to six years, and had attracted a large number of students. The chairman was displeased, but as he was not popular among his colleagues, he was overridden and my name was also put on the ballot. I received four out of five votes. Only Professor Clapp voted against me.

This news was gratefully received. Finally, after so many years of waiting, I had a chance at having work that was both a mission and would also provide me some security. I could not continue as I had been doing. My body was beginning to crack under the strain.

My confidante warned me that "higher authorities" still had to approve the appointment and hinted that problems might arise. Indeed, when the chairman informed me of my appointment he told me that it was only a one year appointment, (failing to mention, of course, that the committee had been told that it was a tenure track). Gertrude Delahunt informed me that Professor Clapp had been very upset that I received the votes. He decided to join forces with Professor Rosenthal (whom I had unwittingly humiliated three years before and who was not on the voting committee) to go to Shuster and urge him to cancel my appointment: I was accused of spreading Catholicism among my students rather than teaching philosophy, the proof being that several of my students had converted. (That sixty-five percent of Catholic students lost their faith by their senior year, as reported to me by Fr. Herman L. Heide, the chaplain of the Newman Club at Hunter, did not seem to disturb the Catholic president.) This information put Shuster in a state of panic: what a nightmare it would be if it became known that Hunter College was a nursery of Catholicism—the bête noire of liberals. Shuster acquiesced to their request, and informed my chairman that the appointment was changed to a year-long appointment which would end in June, 1954.

In the meantime, a rumor spread that some two-hundred and fifty letters from my students had been sent to the Board of Higher Education to protest the cancellation of my appointment to tenure track. How the students found out is to this day a mystery to me. I had had nothing to do with it. Help came from a totally unexpected source. Joseph B. Cavallaro had recently been appointed chairman of the Board of Higher Education. One evening (in either 1953 or 1954) as I was about to begin teaching, he had the kindness of paying me a visit at Hunter to tell me that he had made an appointment with Shuster. He was carrying a heavy briefcase, packed with the letters of protest from the students, and he intended to show them to President Shuster. Later that evening, he was back on the seventh floor where I was teaching and told me that Shuster had been adamant about this decision but, at the same time, he was forced to acknowledge that I had built quite a reputation for myself. Disappointed that his mission had failed, Cavallaro said, "*é un malcalzone*" (a spicy and unflattering Italian epithet) —"he is a rascal."

The year 1953–1954 was one of the most difficult of my career. I had taken a promotion which two of my colleagues wanted to give to another, and people were on the lookout for excuses to prove to Shuster that I was unworthy to teach in a secular college.

I became a political football. Some people were for me and others against me; personal dislikes and grievances played their roles. I had started teaching a course on existentialism, which was the philosophical "fad" of the time (soon to be replaced by analytic philosophy), and my competitor had written his dissertation on Kierkegaard and Heidegger. Thanks to my knowledge of both French and German, I could read the literature that was not yet available in English, and I taught the first course on existentialism offered by Hunter in the fall of 1953.

While teaching it, I felt a strange antagonism rumbling in the classroom. A few of the students who were sitting together began whispering to one another, constantly interrupting and plainly intending to make life miserable for me. I was informed confidentially that a protest against my appointment had been lodged on the basis that I was not teaching philosophy, but rather injecting religion into my teaching. This was "offensive" to the ethos of a city university, which was committed to a strict separation of church and state. There were rumors that several of my students had become Roman Catholics, and that among them there were some Jewish students. This was particularly offensive at Hunter, which was heavily influenced by liberal Jews. The irony is that the real offense was conversion to Roman Catholicism. To become a Buddhist or a Muslim or even a liberal Protestant would largely have been ignored.

But the price of conversion to Catholicism was often greatest for the converts themselves. I remember a Jewish girl who converted whose mother was so upset that she not only went to protest to President Shuster, but also threw her daughter out of the house. The girl came to me in a state of desperation because she had nowhere to live. I arranged for her to stay for a time with my sister and brother-in-law.

It appeared that an attempt was being made to organize a "spontaneous" student protest that there might be "objective" reasons for confirming the cancellation of my appointment. Once, quite accidentally, I saw five or six of the most troublesome students rush from the classroom to meet with Dr. Rosenthal, the professor whom I had unwittingly offended three years before. They were obviously uncomfortable that I had happened to bump into the group and stopped talking in a way that betrayed their conspiratorial ends.

The course on existentialism, in which I focused especially on Kierkegaard, was essentially a historical course. In a sense, to teach historical courses is easier than teaching systematic ones because the philosopher under consideration speaks for himself. In spite of my scholarly approach, however, it was clear that I stood for the objectivity of truth. There is a French proverb that says, "He who wishes to get rid of his dog will accuse him of having the plague." As soon as I mentioned the word "truth" or the word "God" (inevitable when teaching Kierkegaard), the conspirators thought they had a case and hastened to report it to the professor who was inciting them. How is one supposed to teach a course on Kierkegaard without mentioning God?

I might have been tempted to dismiss these thoughts of a protest as the product of an overwrought imagination, but quite accidentally my suspicions were confirmed by a Jewish student in the Kierkegaard course. She appeared in my roster as a "special student," being from another college. She was friendly and quiet, but never came to see me or talk to me. I only knew her name and her face. Once she graduated, I had no more contact with her.

A few months later, I was walking along Madison Avenue toward Hunter, when I ran into this former student. I recognized her and she greeted me, almost passed me by, and then suddenly, turning back, saying, "Professor Jourdain, I have always wanted to tell you something, but I didn't dare to as long as I was a student. Now that I've left Hunter, I feel I must tell you that you were being spied on. It was when I took your course in existentialism. Several students were told to take your class and then to report to one of the professors on the content of your lectures. They had been told you were spreading religion and accused you of doing so every time you mentioned the word 'God.' One day, as I was going down the hall, I overheard several of these girls informing the professor that you were using the classroom as a platform for your religious views. I protested and said to him, 'Professor, I'm also taking this course. This isn't true.' He snapped at me, 'Shut up.' I thought you should know this.'*

The atmosphere during this time was loaded and unbearable. Had I been cleverer in a worldly sense, I should have made a point of greeting my "enemy," flattering him, seeking his advice, and asking for his support.

To many professors terms like "God," "truth," and "objective moral values," were all religious concepts and hence illegitimate in the classroom. They believe, passionately, that one should endorse a democratic "pluralism" of views, and make it clear that everyone has his own god, or no god at all, and that the questions of truth and moral values are matters of opinion. There is one absolute dogma in the liberal world, namely the universal relativity and subjectivity of all values. To challenge this dogma is already to violate the separation of church and state.

Hopefully, I never said in the classroom anything that clashed with my faith, but I definitely refrained from ever mentioning (much less using) arguments borrowed from it. This would have disqualified me as philosopher. I do recall that once in my career, I challenged a student who—out of a clear blue sky—had declared to the class that Catho-

---

* I had suspected it, of course, but here was the proof. I could have used the words of Don Basilio in Mozart's The Marriage of Figaro, with the same tinge of irony, "Ah! Del paggio quel che ho detto/ Era solo un mio sospetto..." ("Ah, what I said of the page/Was only a suspicion of mine").

lics are the most idiotic people in the world. Her argument
was that if it was pouring rain, and the Pope declared that
the sun was shining, they must believe him; otherwise they
would commit a sin.

I told her that she was quite misinformed, and that
Catholics must give their assent to a Pope's teaching only
when spoken ex cathedra on matters of faith and morals.
I could not allow this idiotic assertion to remain unchal-
lenged. It gives some idea of the anti-Catholicism that was
rampant in my classroom.

❧

Soon, a new, clearly well-organized, campaign was launched
against me. The new accusation was that my approach to
aesthetics was so narrow that some students had (suppos-
edly) complained to the art department, which filed a protest with the philosophy department. I was accused of
having condemned nudes in art as immoral and, as one
who was obviously incompetent in the field of aesthetics,
was no longer allowed to teach the course.

I was absolutely flabbergasted. The accusation was
a lie. The basis of the complaint was most likely my distinction between "nudity" and "nakedness," the former
expressing the beauty of the human being, the second
marked by lewd body language which degrades the dignity of the human body, and as a result, makes it ugly. As
a great art lover, I was fully aware of how beautiful and
noble nudes can be. I challenged this claim and told Professor Clapp that I wanted to defend myself by paying a
visit to the chairman of the art department. He became
hysterical, raised his arms in horror. He told me this would

be the worst move I could possibly make, and forbade me to go. I became convinced that he had made up the whole thing, and was suddenly panicked at the thought that his lie would be detected.

I obeyed, but in hindsight I should have defended myself. For about five years, the course was no longer given to me and it was then dropped altogether because no one else wanted to teach it. Then, one day, I was suddenly again permitted to teach the course as if nothing had ever happened.

CHAPTER 11

Among the many students whom I cannot possibly forget was a student with whom I remained in contact for quite a few years. She took the obligatory Introduction to Philosophy course with me in the fifties and, from the very first day, made a point of interrupting and challenging what I was saying, or raising a constant stream of questions. She was the type of student who makes herself unpopular because she plainly wants to be the center of attention. If the teacher cannot master the situation, the whole class becomes a sort of dialogue between one person and the teacher. All teachers have had to deal with this type of problem and will acknowledge that it is neither easy nor pleasant.

Moreover, this particular student had a light stutter which made her delivery painful for others, but did not seem to bother her. She was very self-assured, very aggressive, and obviously had serious personal problems, although she was certainly very intelligent and seemed to have a real interest in philosophical questions.

This was one of the most strenuous and difficult classes that I have had. Either the student was dissatisfied because she thought that I had cut her short or the others were unhappy because they thought that I paid too much attention to her. Several times I tried to make her understand that I had to deal with forty-five students, not just one, but it made little impression upon her.

I do not know how well I managed, but I certainly was glad when the course was over, because the semester was exhausting. Secretly I hoped that she would not take any more courses with me, as she seemed so very opposed to the objectivity of truth. My wishes were not fulfilled. Not only did she show up the next semester, but she became a philosophy major and actually took every single course I gave. She took metaphysics with me and encouraged the other students "to give me hell," which they did.

One of the great difficulties that I have encountered was to convince students that man is not just a highly developed animal. Anthropology and psychology have convinced many of them that "science" has proved "man is nothing but an animal with a more developed brain", and that a study of animal behavior is a key to an understanding of human behavior. I recall that Hunter almost hired a Yale graduate who had done some "in depth" work on the similarity between rats and men.

When students became unresponsive to rational arguments, I found it helpful to resort to humor and wit. I recall that once, when I was struggling to open my students' eyes to man's metaphysical superiority over animals, a student "proved" that we all descended from apes. To claim that man is superior is "nothing but" pride, the wish to place oneself above others.

My arguments met a wall of opposition, and my words were not even listened to. Suddenly, my French wit came to my rescue. I said to the class, "Suppose that I had a sabbatical and spent a few months in Salt Lake City with the

Mormons to do some research on my ancestry. To my joy, I discover that, way back in the Middle Ages, I descended from a French king. This discovery would please my ego, and in some subtle way, I would let my students understand that I still have some 'blue blood' running in my veins." Addressing the student who had challenged me, I said, "Now you claim that your great, great, great, great-grand-mother jumped from tree to tree in Africa. If it is a scientific fact, I shall accept it, but I would not brag about it." The class erupted in laughter.

I continued, "Let us turn back to our problem. As I have tried to show you that I think very highly of man's ontological dignity, it is quite understandable that I expound on it at length in the classroom. But you happen to be convinced that man is 'nothing but' an animal and this conviction seems to delight you. This is baffling indeed and calls for psychoanalysis." The class roared, and that was the end of the problem.

I survived the course on metaphysics as I had survived other very difficult courses, but that irksome student was back for more. After having taken some nine credits with me, her attitude changed. Instead of systematically oppos-ing whatever I was saying, she had become convinced of the validity of the position I was defending, and though she continued to talk a great deal in class, her remarks were no longer disruptive. On the contrary, she would make a point of defending objectivistic views and refuting other students who were attacking them. She must have taken some seven courses with me, and then she graduated.

I thought that I would never see her again, but several years later I received a letter from Spokane, Washington. It was the same student, informing me that she was in a psychiatric hospital, and wanted to tell me that she recalled my classes with gratitude. She also asked me to send her twelve packages of cigarettes, which, after talking it over with my husband, I did do.

Then came another letter that she was going to get Social Security, but her checks were delayed because she was out West. She asked if I could support her in the meantime. I believe I called Social Security at the time only to discover that she had fabricated her story. Alas, I had come to realize she was so disturbed that she could not be trusted.

There was silence for a while and all of a sudden she was in my office in Hunter, announcing that she wanted to take my courses all over again. I was not happy and tried to find various excuses, but the woman would not take "no" for an answer. She knew that through the years, quite a few people had "dropped in" without registering for my courses. I told her that she could also "drop in" on the condition that she would not interrupt and would keep in mind that I would be saying many things that she knew; she should therefore refrain from answering the questions I would raise in the classroom.

I knew I was in for trouble. Not only did she constantly interrupt me, but she was becoming more and more arrogant (a weakness she had displayed since I first met her) and at some point bluntly suggested that as I had already been teaching for quite a few years, it was time she took over the class.

It was getting to be an unbearable situation. After class, she would walk me to my office where my husband was waiting, as he had for several years been accompanying me to Hunter and staying in my office while I taught. She was very impressed by both his mind and personality. One night when walking me to my car, my husband a few feet behind with another student, she told me that if I were to die, she would marry him! It was on the way to my car that she told me she had entered the Church. She was Jewish. I did not ask questions; one thing was clear: truth had conquered. But I was so concerned about her mental state that I did not manifest my joy as would have been proper under normal circumstances.

I was more and more worried about her state of mind and felt that she was once again close to a crisis. Soon afterwards, as I was teaching a medieval philosophy course, expounding Augustine's view of "eternal verities," following Augustine's example, I took a mathematical proposition to exemplify his stand. Suddenly she said, at the top of her voice, "Professor Jourdain, what you say is completely wrong. Two and two make five and I want to prove it to the class."

I had no choice but to ask her to leave, which she did very reluctantly. She rushed to my office and stayed with my husband. I am glad that I did not know this at the time because I would have been so worried that I could not have taught. All of a sudden, there was a loud screaming in the hall. There she was, accusing my husband of having stolen her purse. I had to get in touch with security and the last I saw this tragic girl, she was being led away by a policeman to Bellevue hospital.

In the meantime, I found out that her mother had spent most of her life in an insane asylum. It was one, but not the only, tragic case which I experienced in Hunter. I have had several students who were severely disturbed and I know of three who were interned. When one hears about the background of many of these students, one marvels at the fact that they have the courage to attend college. It is particularly tragic that several of these disturbed people were remarkably talented and doing promising work.

While teaching in the Bronx buildings, I recall a very bright Jewish student who I truly enjoyed teaching. She was the type of student who challenges a teacher to give his or her best. She took a couple of courses with me, though the range of courses I gave in the Bronx building was limited, and one fine day she told me that she was going to graduate, thanking me for my courses.

I experienced what I was going to experience so many more times in my career: the sadness of losing a dear student. First you get to know them, then you get attached. You rejoice over their development, and then all of a sudden they leave to swim in the immense sea of the world. You never know whether you will see them again.

She was one I never saw again, but shortly afterwards, when I was giving another course, in evening session, I noticed while calling the roll that the same surname appeared on the roster. I paid no particular attention to it because certain Jewish names are common, but after class, an attractive, friendly young man came to me and said, "I am taking your class because my sister told me to do so."

He was not as dynamic as his sister, but he was also a good student and I enjoyed having him. He, too, took a couple of courses with me and then graduated. In the meantime, I had been "fired" from day session and was only teaching at Hunter downtown. I started another session of Introduction to Philosophy and once again I saw the same surname on my roll.

After class, the woman who had this last name came to see me. "Dr. Jourdain, my kids told me to take your course." She was definitely no intellectual but she had a sharp mind and a solid common sense. She had probably spent her life raising children and keeping a house, but had a great deal of wisdom and it was refreshing to have her. Everything she said (and she liked to talk) was genuine and based on experience.

One day, she came to see me, and, out of the blue she said, "Dr. Jourdain, do you know that you are a goy?"

A goy! I was a bit shaky because it sounded ominous. I did not have the faintest idea of what it could be. She read my ignorance on my face and explained that it meant I did not belong to the Jewish race, which happens to be true. For Christmas, she gave me a book of Jewish stories which I thoroughly enjoyed because of its wit, even though it was not, as expected, very flattering to the goyim.

CHAPTER 12

From 1953 to 1954, I taught for the last time in day session. In the spring, I requested an audience with President George Shuster, and ask him point-blank why my valid appointment to the tenure track had been cancelled and replaced by a one-year appointment.

"Why was I subjected to this sort of treatment?" I asked. Shuster was ill at ease. He was not enjoying my visit and, perversely, I enjoyed his not enjoying it. "Well, your teaching is strongly marked by your Catholic background," he responded. "You now find yourself in a secular institution, which has another approach to philosophical problems and I personally think that you would be more effective and happier in a Catholic institution." This was a polite way of saying, "You do not belong here." So much for all that high-minded talk about "academic freedom."

I remarked that my defense of the objectivity of truth and of moral values was a highly respectable philosophical position defended by the two greatest "pagan" philosophers, Plato and Aristotle. I could hardly be accused of injecting Catholicism into my teaching merely because I stood up for the objectivity of truth, a position which I supported with purely rational arguments.

He could not answer that objection. He nevertheless insisted that my way of doing it was tainted by Catholicism and that was objectionable in a secular institution.

I remarked that my students did not seem to think so. Many of them were not Catholics and yet they kept taking my courses. Had I fallen into the "sin" to which he referred, it would not explain my success in the classroom.

He grinned and repeated his statement that I did not belong in the city system. I then told him a story of something that had happened to me some time back on a Fifth Avenue bus. I was always reading on my long commute through the city and had with me Joseph Maréchal's book, The Point of Departure of Metaphysics. It was not easy reading and I was completely absorbed by the text, but became conscious that the person sitting next to me was leaning more and more over me. Finding this increasingly disruptive, I looked up to find an elderly woman wearing a straw hat in winter who looked at me with horror and said, "What, you too are one of those awful mystics!" She had confused metaphysics and mysticism. "Mr. President," I added, "Aren't those accusing me of interjecting Catholicism into my courses falling into a similar confusion?"

He laughed uneasily. "I shall be very honest with you. Your colleagues don't want you." Then he added with a fatherly tone, "Take my word for it, you would not be happy in the day session, being unwanted." I told him that I was well aware of who objected to me in the department. "I am speaking to you as a friend," he insisted. "Suppose you stayed in day session. Your life would be miserable. To be rejected by one's colleagues is not pleasant." But, as I was such an "outstanding teacher," he suggested that I move altogether to the evening session.

I answered, "Mr. President, I teach the very same things after sundown. If my teaching is not acceptable when the

sun shines, it is difficult to understand why it should be so
when it sets, for I shall teach the very same thing at night."
He had a wry smile on his face. The poor man excused
himself citing another appointment.

I was defeated, but at least I had fought courageously.
I was a bit shaken but, like Kierkegaard, I was convinced
that "truth must suffer."* It was worth the battle and I
stayed on the job. Now my noble task became to transform defeat into a victory.

I forgot to mention that years earlier (1950), I had
received a private telephone call from President Shuster,
telling me that he had heard I was an outstanding teacher
and had just received a call from the president of a Penn-
sylvania university which was looking for a talented teacher
to be chairman of his philosophy department. "I immediately thought of you," he told me.

I was amazed. I marveled that he had heard about my
work. I was only an insignificant and underpaid teacher
who had been teaching for some eighteen months. I
declined his offer, while thanking him profusely, but I had
the stupidity of telling him that having now experienced
a secular university I was convinced there was a great deal
of work to be done in the secular world which seemed to
be ruled by relativism and subjectivism, and that the challenge attracted me. I would prefer to devote my life to that
sort of work. I could not have said anything more stupid.
This is precisely what he feared. It is only later that I understood how naive I had been to assume that he was trying
to help me.

---

* The Point of View, p. 52.

Instead of being fired altogether, I was relegated to evening session. Evidently, Shuster hoped I would not stay there long: the pay was too low; there was no security, no promotion, and no future.* But I did stay, for the remainder of my academic career.

Another tenure track opened in day session. Thanks to Cavallaro's accusation that Shuster was discriminating against the appointment of Catholics at Hunter, he found a graduate from the University of Chicago who was a Thomist and a Catholic and had the great advantage of having received his diploma from a secular university. His name was William Bryar. The kind Gertrude Delahunt decided to take Bryar under her wings, and informed him about my incredible difficulties. He dreaded sharing my fate, and learned to be "prudent" in his teaching, spending most of his time examining a sentence of Aristotle in the light of various scholarly opinions. He carefully avoided the question of truth, and therefore he was well-treated. He received tenure after three years without a hitch.

---

* In her famous book, *School of Darkness*, Bella Dodd, confirms the systemic injustices at Hunter. She writes, "I had not been back at Hunter long before I found myself involved in discussions on the economic problems of the staff below professorial ranks. Many instructors and other staff members were underpaid and had no security or tenure or promotion" (New York: P. J. Kennedy & Sons, 1963), 62. My husband and I met Dodd in the fall of either 1965 or 1966. She was then famous for her break with Communism which she had once ardently served. It cannot be denied that the efforts of leftists were crucial in the rectification of injustices at Hunter.

(Above) With my mother in the garden of our summer home in Duin-bergen at the Belgian coast. (Below) Learning to use a bicycle (with two wheels in the back for security!) in 1928.

My uncle, Charles van de Vorst, SJ, was the fifth son of his parents. His father, a fallen away Catholic, who became an active free Mason, had married a very pious Catholic girl. He refused to have his children baptized. When expecting Charles, my great grandmother had a very difficult pregnancy, and my grandfather feared she might die. He went to her bedside: "Hélène, what can I do for you?" Without a moment's hesitation, she said, "Albert, if I give you more children, I want them to be baptized and sent to Catholic schools." Not only did she survive, but she gave birth to five more children. Charles was baptized and attended Catholic schools, and eventually became provincial of the Jesuits in Belgium. In 1942, my uncle was a frontrunner to become "Black Pope" (the head of the Jesuits), but the election could not be held because of the War. When the election did take place in 1946, he was no longer eligible since he was over 75 at that point. But his closest associate, Father Janssens, became black Pope, and called my uncle to Rome as his adviser. My uncle died there in 1955. I was told later that he either baptized, or gave the last sacraments to my grandfather, Albert, who died in 1942. I recall that, as a little girl, I put a miraculous medal in my grandfather's pillow case when I visited him in Antwerp.

(Above) Robert Jourdain, SJ, was the youngest child of Louis Jourdain. He joined the Jesuits during the First World War. During our flight from the approaching Nazis, he left Belgium with us in May 1940 before we parted in Moulins. He managed to reach England and became chaplain of the French and Belgian forces during World War II. He accepted a most dangerous mission: to be parachuted into Belgium. He left Belgium and went all through France, but was arrested in Spain and held at the camp in Miranda. Through political maneuvers, he was brought to Gibraltar, and then flown back to England. He received the highest honors from England, France, and Belgium. He died a young, unsung hero in 1955. (Below) 1929 From left to right: me, my brother, and my older sister in school uniform.

My mother and father. They were married on February 26, 1920.

On the day of my confirmation in 1934.

My graduation from grammar school in 1932. I am carrying my school prize: books.

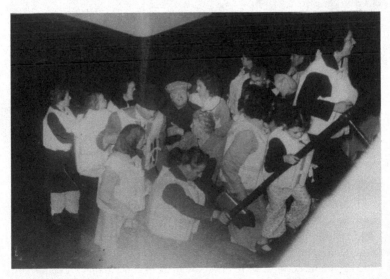

June 11 1940: Our ship, the *SS Washington*, is intercepted by a Nazi submarine. When my sister and I arrived on deck, the life boat that was assigned to us—number 10— was full to capacity. This photo was taken on deck. I am just to right of the man in the cap, who is looking at the camera.

My maternal grandfather, Albert van de Vorst, a maritime lawyer, with his oldest five grand children (the first granddaughter, born some ten years earlier died in infancy). From left to right: The "big" boy is my brother, Robert (Bob), born on January 1, 1921. He died in a tragic car accident (he had six children) in May 1961. The second is my cousin Marc Henry, born in June 1922. He was a pilot in the Belgian army and died in a plane crash in 1950. I am the baby in the middle. I was born on March 11, 1923. Next is my older sister, Marie Helene (Louloute) born in January 1922. She is still alive. She lived in the USA for quite a few years, but is now back in Belgium. She has four children. Last is Marc Henry's sister, Hélène van der Mensbrugghe (a solid Flemish name!). Nicknamed Nenette, she was born on June 21, 1921 and is still living.

Me in the summer of 1941 during our annual trip with my aunt and uncle to Stockbridge, MA. This photo captures my profound unhappiness during those years.

Louloute (left) and I in Central Park in 1942 with our aunt Laure Jourdain Brunner (right) during our stay of several years with her at the Waldorf Astoria.

I was by far the youngest of my class—25 months younger than one of my friends and 18 months younger than the other.

Louloute and I in front of the building at 526 West 113th Street where we lived after we left the Waldorf, Photo taken in 1947.

From 1962 to 1964, my husband and I were invited to Mexico several times to give talks. This picture was taken during our trip in 1962.

Crossing a lake in southern Bavaria on a windy day in the late 1950s.

Receiving an award at the chancery in the 1960s from Msgr. John J. Voight, Secretary of Education for the Archdiocese of New York.

With Gabriel Marcel in 1960.

My husband Dietrich and I shortly after our marriage. We are in our apartment at 448 Central Park West at 105th Street (Harlem begins at 110th). This photo was taken in our dining room (i.e. the corridor leading to the living room).

In Salzburg in the 1960s.

In Puerto Rico in the early 1960s. My husband had been invited to give a talk.

Just outside of Florence, Italy in 1969.

Meeting with Pope John Paul II in January 1980.

(Above) With Pope Benedict XVI on March 26, 2007. (Below) In 2013, Pope Francis granted me the title Dame Grand Cross of the Pontifical Equestrian Order of St. Gregory. Here I receive the insignia of the Order at the hands of my revered friend, Raymond Cardinal Burke.

503 East Lake Ave.
Baltimore, Md. 21212
September 27, 1972

To whom it may concern:

Students in e82.84 - Introduction to Philosophy ~~xxxxxxxxxxxxxxxx~~ ~~xxxxxxx~~ ~~xxxxxx~~ xxxxxxx, were advised by the instructor, publicly, that they should avoid taking courses with Dr. Alice Jourdain, a colleague of his at that time. There seemed to be no direct communication between the two instructors, nor was there ever any indication that he knew her personally.

Winifred Neville

Proof that other professors at Hunter were actively trying to persuade students not to take my classes.

The President's Award for Excellence, which I received in 1984.

Receiving an Honorary Doctorate from Franciscan University of Steubenville in 1988.

CHAPTER 13

B y the fall of 1954, as already mentioned, I was permanently relegated to the School of General Studies. After seven years of successful teaching, I was still a lecturer. My academic future was bleak, and it was clear to me that the president and many of my colleagues hoped the evening session would motivate me to leave. Yet after seven incredibly trying years, I was convinced that I was doing meaningful work. I now felt equipped to address the innumerable nationalities, the wide range of philosophical outlooks, and the most various of backgrounds, particularly the humble and problematic circumstances typical of Hunter College students.

I will forever be grateful to some professors outside of the philosophy department who came to my aid. But one's friends are not always as dedicated as one's enemies. For example, I found in my files the following letter written by the chairman, Professor O'Gorman, and dated January 22, 1954, "I have observed Dr. Alice Jourdain. I think I can say without serious contradiction that she is probably the best teacher in the Philosophy Division of our department. The students constantly desire to get into her sections. She displays a thorough knowledge of her subjects and handles her classes with the greatest poise. She is undoubtedly one of our most gifted teachers." As genuinely appreciative as this letter was, and as desirable as it might have been in

another setting, Professor O'Gorman's praise probably did
me more harm than good.

The letters sent by my former Fordham Professors were
all very positive. My trump card was a letter from the famous
Werner Jaeger. I had the good fortune of meeting this distinguished scholar when I was a young student studying
for my PhD comprehensive during a stay with friends in
Vermont. Jaeger happened to have a cottage nearby. Not
only did I get to know him, I had the privilege of having
several talks with him, and questioned him about Plato, to
my mind, the greatest of Greek philosophers. I was particularly interested in the philosophical and moral influence
of Socrates on Plato. At the end of the *Phaedrus*, Plato says
of Socrates, "he was the wisest and justest man I met in my
life." I knew that one cannot understand Plato without the
figure of Socrates, even though Plato would dwarf his men-
tor, and so I asked Jaeger for intellectual guidance. He was
most kind and enjoyed both my youthful enthusiasm and
my devotion to this gigantic thinker. He had the kindness
of writing a recommendation letter for me, based on our
private conversations, and my department chair showed it
to me, handwritten on a piece of pale blue paper written in
a beautiful European cursive. I discovered a few years later,
when finally I applied for tenure, that the letter had mysteriously disappeared from my file. The matter was never
clarified, as a teacher's files are supposed to be locked, available only to the members of the faculty who are on the
Personnel and Budget Committee. To this day, I have no
doubt that the letter was destroyed by one of my colleagues.

So life went on. I set my mind upon developing the
philosophy department of the evening session into some-

thing respectable and was encouraged by the number of students who started taking a whole series of courses with me. They would begin with the Introduction to Philosophy and then take three, four, or five more courses. Around this time, in the late 1950s, philosophy was introduced as a major during evening session, and to my joy, quite a few students chose this course of study. The many students who flocked to my classes were a primary reason the major could be offered in the evening. It was also encouraging to see students who had done poorly in day session suddenly pick up interest and, carried by true intellectual enthusiasm, begin doing very good work in evening session.

I devoted my love and care to grooming the "miserable garden" to which I had been assigned. Some evening students were very bright and very talented and I made the best of it, working to transform the evening session from an insignificant appendix of the college into a department in its own right, offering a variety of courses and attracting some outstanding students. I taught six courses in the fall in 1954, and still managed to publish several articles and do some translation work. At the end of that year I had earned $3,812.20. I learned to live very frugally. It is amazing what one can endure when one has a sense of mission.

I remember a class of Introduction to Philosophy downtown in evening session. The class was filled to capacity. At this point in time the course was obligatory, and there were quite a few students who had no interest in the course but had to take it.

It was relatively early in my career and I was using a much higher, European standard of grading: an "A" meant absolutely outstanding work. I found out that my colleagues were marking much more generously than I was and through the years, because the standards have gone down so terribly, I had to grow more "generous." At any rate, for this class, I found to my sorrow, after correcting midterm exams, that I could only give one "A." I did not know the student who had done well, but I discovered him when I returned the tests.

The student seemed in heaven and rushed to me after class, "Dr. Jourdain, I am deliriously happy. I took philosophy in the Bronx buildings and got an 'F', and for this reason, lost my matriculation and am now in evening session working toward regaining it. I hated the course up there. The professor never truly taught, but sat way back in the classroom and would throw out a theme and let the students discuss whatever they wanted. It was sheer bedlam and one could not learn anything serious. But a clique of admirers surrounded him and they were the only ones who received As. Now, I truly have discovered what philosophy is like and I love it."

He took about five courses with me and did beautifully in each one of them, even though he was a chemistry major. That gave me joy. I had a similar experience with another girl who had been "fired" from day session because of poor work. She told me that she was so bored that she did not care. She took all the courses that I was giving, however, and was one of my very first philosophy majors in evening session. She turned out to be an exceptional student.

Over the years, many students would open up to me about their problems and struggles. I recall a tragic case, a young woman who was taking my classes but never said a word in them. She was very withdrawn and I cannot recall that she ever came to see me in my office as many other students did. Afterwards, she disappeared and I never had much of a chance to talk to her.

One fine day, I found a note from her under the door of my apartment, telling me how much my courses had helped her and that they had shed a bit of light in the darkness of her life. (I never found out how she found my address since the contact information for professors at Hunter was never made public.) What could I do but to thank her? Unfortunately, that seemed to give her a certain license and she developed the catastrophic habit of calling me at home. I taught until ten at night, four times a week, and rarely came home before eleven at night, dead tired. The student did not live far from the college and had calculated how long it would take me to come home. Sometimes she would phone and start to tell me her problems the moment I walked in the door. At another time, she called me at two in the morning.

The poor woman came from a broken home and when she was only twelve years old, her father took her to bars to teach her to drink. She left home young, fell among the seamiest people, and had gone through a lot in her life, but these daily telephone calls, lasting for indefinite lengths of time, were not only a great strain but were also meaningless. It took me some time to realize that she was often drunk and needed professional help.

She refused to attend Alcoholics Anonymous, but I learned that she had a great admiration for a priest who had done social work in South America and happened to be Belgian. I knew about him because he had written an excellent book against Nazism and found out that he would be coming to New York. Together, with several generous and charitable friends, we devised a plan and went to the dirty and miserable flat of this troubled woman, attempting to talk her into going to a place where she might be rehabilitated. The moment we touched upon the theme of her problem, however, she closed up and I knew we had lost.

That same night, she called me and piled up reproaches upon me. She felt that she had been betrayed and that was the last I heard from this poor girl. A few years later, I found out through another student who happened to work in a laboratory that she was stealing pure alcohol and drinking it. That was one of the many tragic experiences that I had at the city university, where a high percentage of students had very serious personal problems. Yet they would never accept the help that Hunter offered, feeling they were treated as "cases" instead of persons.

Back in the early 1950s, I had suggested to the chairman that he introduce an Introduction to Philosophy course in evening session. He agreed; he was taking no risk. If registration were insufficient, the course would simply be dropped. However, it turned out to be a resounding success, with fifty students registered, requiring us to be transferred to a larger room. Now I introduced a course on social philosophy which attracted many students. In 1955, I introduced metaphysics for the first time in evening session. Finally, I introduced a course in medieval philosophy, which was an act of daring for the plain reason that the main accusation leveled against me was that I was proselytizing in the classroom. The course had quite a bit of success and I continued to give it every second or third year.

In the spring of 1955, Professor Clapp informed me

that I could no longer teach so many courses (more than the fifteen standard hours), because "it was too exhausting" and I could not possibly do a good job teaching so many hours. It sounded so paternal and so kind. I knew, however, that several day session professors who taught a full schedule in the day gave additional courses in the evening. I remarked timidly that it would be difficult for me to live on five courses, and I could not help but notice it was precisely his hope that starvation would force me out of Hunter. The real concern still seemed to be that as more and more students were flocking to my classes, some limit needed to be placed on my "nefarious" influence. I have always believed it was for this reason that my very popular course on social philosophy was dropped.

I learned another lesson. My years at the city university taught me that in many apparently "innocent" decisions, there is more than meets the eye. For instance, anyone acquainted with class registration knows that the best hours for the students are generally the earlier ones. Only those who have no alternative take the latest courses at 8:45. Many of the evening session students worked during the day. They had to curtail food and sleep and endure getting home very late. Not only is it often dangerous, but as buses and subways run on a slower schedule, it takes much longer to go back home after eight or nine o'clock. By giving me later classes, chances were that I would get fewer students—although I'm pleased to report there were never any problems on that score: the students still swarmed to my classes.

Soon I found out that the inventiveness of the delegate chairman had a very wide range. As he had prohibited me from giving more than five courses, I was hoping that twice a week, my schedule would allow me to leave Hunter shortly after eight thirty, instead of ten at night. I made this request, and should have expected that it would be turned down. I was given an early class, then a break of an hour-and-a-half, and then the late course ending at ten. What was I to do? I had no office of my own, and I was still sharing my colleague's desk.

In fact, I once overheard him advising a younger teacher, who was trying his hand at arranging schedules for the first time. He told the younger teacher that if he wanted to get rid of another professor, he should ask him what schedule is most convenient for him. And then write him a note that he could not be accommodated. That, he said, was the easiest way of getting rid of undesirable teachers. To this very day, it is difficult for me to understand why he nourished this subtle hatred toward me, who had never antagonized him.

I decided to use my time intelligently and found in the Hunter catalogue that a course of Italian literature was being offered during my "free" time. I did not hesitate, and asked the professor if I might sit in his class. He was very friendly and although the course was too advanced for the Italian I had picked up on the streets of Florence, I enjoyed the challenge and followed that course with six others, gaining a fair command of the beautiful tongue of Dante. In a small way, these hours devoted to Italian allowed me a defeat into victory. It was clear that I would never enjoy all the privileges attached to a day session appointment but, on the other hand, being relegated to the evening session, I no longer had to travel between Hunter downtown and Hunter uptown.

CHAPTER 14

No one is as illiberal as a liberal. I recall the Hunter student newspaper once printed an article claiming that "all religions should be welcome," but that none should lay claim to be the true one. It suggested that Orthodox Jews should give up their claim that they were God's Chosen People, and Roman Catholics their claim to have the fullness of revealed truth. Then the world would be at peace. The city colleges claimed to welcome all ideas and encourage unconditionally what was called "broad-mindedness," yet in practice anyone deemed "narrow-minded" was vulnerable to the most exquisite intolerance.

I was left in peace, up to a point, at least. I recall that the primary antagonist among my colleagues visited my class in the late 1950s to write a report on my performance. It was a most unpleasant experience. He came a few minutes late, and left ten minutes early. Today, when an adjunct's class is visited, the teacher must be advised days in advance so that he can prepare himself particularly well. He is entitled to read the report written on his teaching and can write a rebuttal and defend himself if his evaluation is negative. But at that time, there were no such warnings. All of a sudden, this professor came, sat in the class with an unfriendly face, and made a point of taking notes. His written report was hidden in the mysterious files of the department, accessible only to people on committees. I found out through the grapevine that these reports were devastatingly critical of me. Roman Catholicism was clearly his bête noire. Not only was I a Catholic; moreover, I had the reputation of taking my religion seriously.

This disease was epidemic, and certainly not limited to Hunter. When a classmate of mine, Betty McCormack, became president of Manhattanville College of the Sacred Heart in the 1960s, she proclaimed in her inaugural address that, ". . . from now on, all ideas will be welcome at Manhattanville." She kept her word. In short order this once profoundly Catholic college was totally secularized.

Once I commented in the classroom that it was puzzling that broad-minded people should have no room in their minds for narrow-minded people, whereas it was understandable that a narrow-minded person cannot endorse the views of a broad-minded one. According to this incomprehensible viewpoint, it is broad-minded to take a purely sociological view of ethics à la Margaret Mead. It is narrow-minded to claim that certain actions are intrinsically evil. A colleague of mine by the name of Professor Ross Harrison, a psychologist, who happened to travel from Hunter downtown to Hunter uptown with me, once said to me that it is "sheer arrogance to claim that one knew what was objectively good and objectively evil." Apparently he did not recognize the supreme irony of the question that remained, "Is not arrogance, then, objectively evil?"

Appeals to "academic freedom" are also often marked by similar irony. There is no limit to one's right to speak about many points of view and many interpretations; but to teach that a particular position is true, that in turn is a violation of academic freedom. I remember a faculty meeting during which my colleagues discussed what should be covered in Introduction to Philosophy. I suggested that the question of truth be made a primary topic to which one of my colleagues responded, "whose truth?" Some of my colleagues snickered. I should have asked, "whose freedom?"

The following occurred in 1955. The first time I taught metaphysics, a woman in her forties, Winifred Neville, was taking the course. She sat in the back of the room, never saying a word, but apparently enjoying the classroom drama. I had a very bright bunch of "liberal" students who had ganged up together and decided (as Winifred later reported) "to give her hell." This was not the first time I had heard these words.

They did. As soon as they suspected that one of my arguments might lead to the spirituality of the human soul or to the existence of the First Cause, they played a game of interrupting me, shouting me down, ridiculing what I was saying, and offering shallow rebuttals. It was one of the most exhausting courses I have given in my life. With a lot of prayers, and God's grace, I survived, but when I left the classroom, I was absolutely drained.

One day, Winifred met me in the hall after the completion of the course and told me that she had admired my courage through this very trying semester. Out of the blue, she said, "Do you know why I decided to take your class?" I said I had not the faintest idea. "Because I had been told not to," she answered. I was amazed. "I took Introduction to Philosophy with another professor," she proceeded. (In fact, he was a recently appointed adjunct). This was a young man (I believe his name was Cornish) who only had his MA and whom I had never met personally as our schedules did not overlap. "When the course was over, he told the class that he hoped he had convinced us that philosophy could be challenging and interesting. It also was his hope that some of us would take other courses; however, he gave us a caveat, "Don't ever take any of the courses of Dr. Jourdain."

That remark sent the student directly to the Hunter College catalog, where she looked up my background and read that I had my BA from Manhattanville College and my MA and PhD from Fordham University—both Catholic institutions. As a practicing Catholic, she decided to take my course on metaphysics and thought it was her duty to warn me that I was being not only discriminated against, but openly maligned. She even gave me a notarized statement testifying to the amazing behavior of the young adjunct who must have obeyed an order given from "above" (since he did not even know me).

In the meantime, I had had the joy of seeing Dietrich von Hildebrand's Ethics published in early 1953. Convinced of his extraordinary gifts and seeing that he was perpetually in the red, I approached the publisher P. J. Kenedy and proposed a new volume that would gather some of his best essays. Kenedy responded favorably, while asking us to increase the selection we had proposed. The book appeared in 1953 under the title The New Tower of Babel. I continued my collaboration with von Hildebrand in two important books on ethical themes. True Morality and Its Counterfeits,* which appeared in 1955, addressed

---

* This important book is also known by the title of its second edition, *Morality and Situation Ethics*, which appeared in 1966.

the growing problem of relativism in ethics, while Graven Images, published 1957, returned to the theme of "value blindness" and explored the countless attitudes and dispositions that can cloud our minds and our consciences. These studies were needed when they were written. They have since become indispensable.

CHAPTER 15

Around the year 1956, another tenure track position opened in the philosophy department and, as expected, my name was not put on the slate. A young man by the name of William Klubach, who had just received his degree from Columbia, got the job, and even though lacking experience, received a starting salary much higher than mine, which was still hourly after almost seven years of teaching. We were told that he was exceptionally talented and promised to be one of the lights of the department.

Exiled in evening session, I did not make his acquaintance right away but finally met him at a faculty meeting. He had a great deal of self-assurance. As soon as a problem was discussed in the department, he offered a solution. This was a bit presumptuous from someone who had only been at the college a few months.

I also was told that he was an extraordinary linguist. As I have a great interest in languages, I tested his knowledge and discovered that his "command" of French, German, and Italian fell far short of his reputed abilities. In our department, it was not difficult to impress people with foreign languages. Apart from Professor Somerville, who spoke perfect Russian, no one had any competence in a foreign tongue.

I hardly ever saw Klubach, but heard that he was making a name for himself. After three years, he applied for tenure and suddenly there were rumors that he had deeply offended Professor William Bryar by claiming that the value of a PhD from Chicago could not be compared to a PhD from Columbia.

Once again the department was divided into two camps, but tucked away in the evening session, I avoided the fray. I was once asked what I thought of the fellow's linguistic talents and had to respond that, in all honesty, he had limited accomplishments. Then I went on vacation and blissfully forgot about Hunter and its problems.

When I came back, I met a day session colleague who told me, "Have you heard the news?" Of course, I hadn't. "Klubach has been fired!" I was amazed. His career had seemed so promising. What had happened? "It's very simple," I was told. "The Department of Philosophy received a letter from Columbia University, forwarding a copy of a letter written by an Italian scholar who asked Columbia how they could justify granting a PhD to someone whose dissertation had plagiarized from this scholar's book." That was like a bomb. Not only was his degree withdrawn but, of course, the man lost his job.

The battle over Klubach's tenure was clearly not a case of discrimination. The man was cocky and brazen, needlessly offending the feelings of other professors. A professor's personality is not an unimportant factor in college life and may justify opposition. Plagiarism, of course, was a *coup de grâce*.

Another interesting episode involved a man named Morris Philipson, who had a part-time appointment at

Hunter. At the same time he was also working at a major press and suggested that he, along with two colleagues who were particularly antagonistic toward me, should write a textbook for the course on Introduction to Philosophy. He could guarantee that the press where he worked would publish it. Each of them would choose excerpts from various philosophers and write a brief introduction. As Philipson had promised, the book was published.* Philosophy then belonged to the core curriculum, and as Hunter had thousands of students, the book was guaranteed to sell extremely well—and it did. Moreover, it also guaranteed that one of the contributors, who had no publication history, would thereby become eligible to receive a full professorship. Thousands and thousands of copies were bought by the department. The book was bound and quite expensive.

I looked at it, and decided not to use it in my classroom, believing most of the selections to have been poorly made. The choice of the texts ensured that the students would be fed primarily on rationalism, idealism, and empiricism. This did not increase my popularity with my colleagues. To choose Plato's *Sophist*—one of the late and difficult dialogues—struck me as a very unwise choice for beginners. Moreover, the very same texts were available in series called *The Library of Liberal Arts* for sixty cents. Knowing how my students were struggling financially, I found it immoral to foist upon them an expensive textbook.

Once again, there was a vacancy in the Department of Philosophy, and another young man who had gradu-

---

* *Foundations of Western Thought Six Major Philosophers Plato, Aristotle, Descartes, Berkeley, Hume, Kant* (New York: Alfred Knopf, 1964).

ated from Columbia a few years previously, who had been
teaching at City College, was appointed the position. His
name was Michael Wyschogrod, the very same person who,
in 1953, had been selected by Shuster, and whose appointment I had unwittingly blocked by being voted in myself.
Being in evening session, I did not get to know him well
for quite a while, but at one point our schedules were
arranged so that we shared an office and had an occasional
opportunity to chat.

To my joy, I found out that he was a believing Jew. He
even informed me that he carefully fulfilled all the Jewish laws. He was European born, had lived in Germany
(although his parents were Hungarian), and his family had
fortunately left Germany and come to the United States
as a young boy. We had various common interests, including a love for classical music. We got along well, and I was
grateful to have a colleague who not only believed in God,
but who, moreover, was courteous and friendly.

In 1957, there was big news. The Board of Higher Education had finally granted three instructors tenure tracks
(the lowest on the scale of appointments) to the evening
session faculty. The question was who would get them.

The evening session faculty was a motley crowd. They
were, for the most part, beginners without PhDs. They
usually stayed only for a short time and then moved on
to better paying work. Evening session was merely a stop
along the way. Then there were a number of day session
teachers who wanted to make additional money. Finally,
there were a handful of distinguished professors who, for
whatever personal reasons favored evening hours. I, myself,
had been at Hunter for ten years at this point, and our list

of philosophy majors in the evening session consisted of seventeen of my students, as compared to the day session, with five majors between all the full-time professors.

So, the slate of possible candidates for the three tenure tracks was limited. Beginners were excluded, as were those without a PhD. The day session professors already had their tenure. So this did not leave very many possibilities. George Shuster gave me one of the three positions, assuaging his bad conscience for having excluded me from day session after 1954.

I had been suffering from a bad knee for years, which gave me constant pain, though the pain varied in quality. In the spring of 1957, the pains became acute and one morning, early in June, I bent down to pick up a fallen handkerchief and my knee locked, blocked by a piece of loose cartilage. The leg was so badly bent that it was impossible to stretch it and the pain was excruciating. Providentially, this awful experience happened as I was standing next to my bed, where I then lay down, bathed in sweat. The phone rang and I heard the voice of Professor Davidson, the Dean of the School of General Studies. His position granted him very little power (as evening session was managed by day session), but I knew he supported me completely. While in this excruciating condition I learned that I had received one of the three tenure track positions as an instructor, with the lowest possible salary.[*]

I do not know how my day session colleagues reacted to the news. At the time, the salary gap between day session and evening session continued to be enormous, with-

---

[*] Still, for the first time, my annual salary would reach the $4,000 mark!

out promotion possibilities or pension benefits. But for the first time after ten years, I was no longer paid by the hour, and that was a significant improvement.

My work was meaningful, but I was always grateful when the summer came, and I could have some respite. This particular summer, I traveled to Munich and underwent surgery on my knee. I had no medical coverage and the rates in Germany were at that time extremely low compared to the United States. However, it was an unsuccessful operation and my knee continued to cause pain and discomfort.

CHAPTER 16

I was still working intensely on Dietrich von Hildebrand's manuscripts. The ten years I had spent in the "liberal" world of Hunter had taught me many things. I had become a sort of "expert" on the relativistic mentality and on the role that "moral substitutes" play in human life. All this was masterfully presented by the man who was my "teacher" in the deepest sense of this term, and with whom I had shared the information I gathered daily in my classroom. That became the key theme of Graven Images, published in 1957.

In 1959, I married Dietrich von Hildebrand. He had been a widower for two years. There was such a perfect understanding between us religiously, spiritually, philosophically, and artistically. We shared the very same outlook, the same ideals, and the same way of life. He had, in a very real way, made me who I had become. However, I decided to keep my maiden name "Jourdain" at Hunter. By that time, I was well-known, and aside from the fact that a German name was hardly a trump card after the war, he was known as an ardent Catholic.

I had now been teaching for twelve years and was to come up for tenure in the fall of 1959. I was informed that, as part of the tenure process, I was to review and update my Curriculum vitae (and it was at that point that I discovered that Werner Jaeger's letter of recommendation was missing from my file.) This necessitated going to Hunter earlier and made it inevitable that I would bump into some of my day session colleagues.

The atmosphere of intrigue was still rampant, which seemed ludicrous to me. I had been relegated to the evening session with a miserable salary and no prospect of promotion. Nevertheless, I had introduced a whole series of new courses in the evening session and all of them had attracted many students. I prepared my dossier carefully and put the whole thing in God's hands.

In January 1960 over the winter break, my husband and I went to California where he had been invited to lecture. When I returned, I found a terse note informing me that I was to report to the dean's office on February 2 at one o'clock in the afternoon. No explanation was given.

A bit apprehensive, I entered the dean's office at the appointed time. Imagine my amazement when I found myself facing not only the deans of both day and evening session but also the heads of Hunter's fifteen departments. All told, I faced a group of seventeen people. I was asked to sit down, and for two hours I was grilled on the content of my teaching: was I teaching that there is such a thing as truth? It was clearly a well-orchestrated, systematic attack designed to trip me up. Some of those present found the entire affair distasteful. But typically, they said little. I do recall the dean, Mina Rees, arguing that what I called the "objectivity of truth" actually meant "my mind agreeing with my mind." I did not dare tell her that that was not a very powerful argument. If "truth" is only "my mind agreeing with my mind," then the word "error" loses any sense. Professor Livingston Welsh, head of the Psychology

Department, finally lost patience and protested, "If there is no objective truth, we had better close up the place."

After two hours, my interrogation was over and I left the college, shaking. For the first time in thirteen years, I could not control my tears and decided to visit my closest friend, Madeleine Froelicher (who in 1959 had married Lyman Stebbins, later the founder of Catholics United for the Faith), rather than go home immediately and upset my husband. There I slowly regained my composure.

But I "made it," narrowly, in a 9-to-8 vote. One colleague informed me that "he had appealed to the jury's pity," and convinced them to confirm my appointment "because I had been there so long that one could no longer decently get rid of me." As I had learned to distrust whatever he said, I found it difficult to believe him. He clearly wanted me to feel indebted to him.

In my naiveté, I believed that everyone at Hunter was grilled before receiving tenure. This "privilege," however, was one for which I had been singled out. I later realized that when other professors came up for tenure, there were no investigations, no special procedures. The department made its recommendations and the Board of Higher Education approved. In my case, when the recommendation for my tenure was sent to the Board of Higher Education, there were protests both in and outside the board. Had I had no success with the students, they could have said that I was ill-equipped to teach, but this was not the case. Moreover, I attracted students from varying backgrounds and had my teaching actually been thinly veiled Catholicism, there would have been vigorous complaints. The students, however, were not the problem. Sometime later at a conference, I happened to see Edward Re (the husband of Peggy Corcoran, who graduated with me at Manhattan-ville in 1944) who was a member of the Board of Higher Education. "Do you believe in miracles?" he asked. "I do, indeed," I answered, to which he said, "Your getting tenure was nothing short of one." Aside from the opposition from within the university, I learned that several liberal rabbis had gone to the board to protest my tenure. It edges on the ridiculous, but it is a fact.

Part of me was tempted to be flattered to receive so much attention. How was it possible that I, an insignificant person, a young girl who came from a foreign country, should arouse the ire of so many august professors? I was both astonished and puzzled and told myself that clearly my defense of objective truth was creating waves.

I have made clear that the city university was ruled by politics. That a Catholic "nobody" like me should trigger such vicious opposition and nevertheless "make it," despite a wall of opposition, shows how it was really God who "appointed" me and who placed me in a position which in natural terms I was ill-equipped to fill. Indeed, He chooses the weak and leads His candidate to victory.

Was I the victim of anti-Catholicism? I am quite conscious of the fact that being a woman was a handicap at that time. But I had a PhD, had given quite a few lectures, and had published. In 1950 I had translated Dietrich von Hildebrand's Fundamental Moral Attitudes from German into English; I had also translated his essay, "The New Functionalism." Indeed, I had for years collaborated with a man who was one of the leading philosophers of the twentieth century. On the other hand, it is possible that my colleagues were aware of my husband's prominence as a Catholic writer, and this of course would not have helped my cause. The only reasonable explanation for my treatment is prejudice—either because of my gender or because of my faith, or both.

Of course, now that I had tenure, life was different. I could no longer be fired and the awful tension of the last thirteen years was partly gone. (I say "partly" because an unwelcome member of a department can be tormented in all sorts of ways, while the person who suffers under these attacks can never "prove" discrimination.) I was still an instructor, and was hoping against hope that, sooner or later, promotion would become possible in evening session.

In fact, the Board of Higher Education finally granted promotions in the School of General Studies in the 1960s. Although I had just obtained my tenure, it seemed that I was entitled to a promotion, too. When I approached the delegate chairman about it, he flew into a rage. I can still see him pulling the shade of his office in Room 726 so brutally that it slipped from his hand and went up with a bang. "You're always pushing and pressing!" he growled and told me I was ruining my chances for promotion instead of having confidence in him and letting him arrange matters. He reminded me that he had favored my tenure by stressing the fact that I deserved pity! (Alas, I had reasons to mistrust his memory.) It was not encouraging. My experience of the last thirteen years made it difficult for me to grant him my confidence. He was the one who a few years earlier had gone to Shuster to convince him to cancel my appointment to a tenured position.

I decided to speak to my friend, Mary R. Sheehan,

professor in Psychology, who had always shown great kindness toward me. All through the difficult years I had spent at Hunter, she had been a great source of moral support through her kindness and thought I was shamefully treated. She went to the dean, told her what I had accomplished in the evening session, and got the promotion for me by going over the delegate chairman's head. That January of 1960, I became an assistant professor, with a modest raise in salary, but still a long way to go to reach a full professorship. In fact, it would take me another eleven years. I know quite a few people who have traveled the same road in one third the time or less. But they belonged to the establishment and reflected the Zeitgeist, that is, they all were going with "the time." The more one's views reflect the spirit of the time, the faster one is promoted. I was definitely swimming against the tide.

These battles and the years of overwork and fatigue took their toll. I was not feeling well and often dragged myself to work. The entire fall semester of 1960 was punctuated by a series of illnesses. I spent many weekends in bed in order to have the strength to work on Mondays. On two occasions my husband taught my classes for me because I was running a fever.

Just before Christmas, I became very seriously ill. I had a virulent bladder infection, all my glands were swollen, and I was running a high fever. I was in bed for four weeks with temperatures running up to 103 degrees. The doctor kept coming, but it took quite a while to diagnose that I had a violent attack of mononucleosis. Dr. Muller told me that my symptoms proved that I had a textbook case of this troublesome disease. I was forced, therefore, to take a sick-leave during the spring semester of 1961.

God had been good to me. Had this happened earlier, having no tenure, I would not have been entitled to a sick-leave and my job certainly would have been given to someone else. I was deeply grateful and saw Providence working.

My husband and I decided to go to the Canary Islands and, for the first time since I left the Waldorf in 1946, I had a real rest. I was so down that I truly needed a prolonged break. We chose the Canary Islands because the peseta was so low against the dollar that one could live in a good hotel with three meals a day for $5.00. That was our cup of tea. Moreover, these beautiful islands were not yet totally ruined by "tourists" who are like locusts in Egypt.

While away, I received a friendly letter informing me that philosophy was to become an autonomous department. The "unhappy" (while for me fortunate) marriage of psychology and philosophy, which had lasted for so many years, was coming to a close. My feelings were mixed. The fact that the Department of Psychology had housed philosophy for so long was, in and of itself, not fortunate. On the other hand, I could not forget that the psychologists were the ones who had been most helpful and friendly toward me. Now that philosophy was to become a separate department, who was going to be the chair? Even though I finally had my tenure, I was still at the mercy of the chair's mood, and I still had a long way to go before reaching a full professorship.

So the philosophy professors moved out of the psychology offices and desks were assigned to the various members of the philosophy department. When I came back at the end of the summer, I found out that I, although I was now assistant professor, I had been assigned no office and therefore no desk of my own, while a brand new faculty member, a man from Syria who was neither a professor nor tenured, had both. Once again, my "enemy" had not forgotten me. Dr. Catherine Reid from psychology had pity on me and allowed me to share her desk. I swallowed the pill, said nothing, and used Dr. Reid's office for several years.

As a regular member of the department, I now had to observe the classes of adjuncts and beginners to evaluate their performance. I did this task for the rest of my academic career. In 1962, I was told to visit the newest member of our faculty who was supposed to be teaching seventeenth century philosophy, as printed in the catalogue. I assumed, therefore, that he would discuss Descartes, Spinoza, and Leibniz. To my amazement, however, he was expounding the philosophy of Hume, and Hume, born in 1711, is not by any stretch of the imagination a seventeenth century philosopher. Nor is Hume a particularly edifying thinker. In the derisive words of Baron von Hügel, "He is the sort of person young people are taken in by. They take him for something else. He knows everything. He got to the bottom of everything when he was sixteen. . . ."*

I noticed that one of my students was taking the course. When I left the classroom, she ran after me, and asked me what I thought about the young teacher's performance. I avoided answering by asking my own questions, "Wasn't he supposed to teach seventeenth century philosophy? What has he been doing until now?" My student responded, "We

* Letter to a Niece, XIII.

are all very disappointed. All that he has done until now is to expound St. Thomas' proofs of God's existence and tear them to pieces, using Hume's arguments."

I was depressed at the thought that the department would be saddled with him for years to come. But my worry was needless: a year or so later, his grandfather died, leaving him a huge inheritance, and he decided to go back to his home country of Syria. As soon as he left, I applied for his office and his desk and I got them. I had waited for a desk of my own for fifteen years.

Another time, I was assigned to sit in the classroom of a young man, recently appointed by my chairman. He sat on his desk, and began his class by informing the students that "John Stuart Mill was the son of Jeremy Bentham." A student raised her hand and inquired, "How is it that father and son have different names?" A pertinent question indeed. The teacher covered his mouth with his hand, and found himself in deep waters. Alas, there are such teachers in places of "higher learning." It reminded me of a lovely woman, Alberta, who for years cleaned my apartment. She was not terribly efficient, but was so lovely that I would never have exchanged her for another. We used to talk, and I always marveled at the soundness of her ideas. One day I could not help but ask her, "Alberta, where did you collect all this wisdom? Without a moment's hesitation, she answered, "You see, Mrs. von Hildebrand, I have not been ruined by education; I left school in the third grade."

CHAPTER 17

In the early 1960s, Hunter's graduate program came into existence. One can well imagine the political eddies this development triggered. It is fascinating to observe how many people long for power and renown. Of course, apart from the prestige, work at the Graduate Center, would also bring better pay. It was clear from the very beginning that to be appointed here became the aspiration of many professors.

Once again, the political devil was loose and there were a lot of mysterious discussions going back and forth. Like all big projects, it had to be started on a small scale and the department first introduced an MA program, which later became a full-fledged PhD program. Ruth Weintraub, a graduate of Hunter and professor of political science, was named Dean of the Graduate Program. Bella Dodd, who knew her from her days as a student at Hunter, told me bluntly that Weintraub was one of my deadly enemies. When I said that I did not know her, she said, "yes, but she knows of you, and being violently anti-Catholic, she will do everything in her power to put obstacles in your path." Dodd was right. Later I met Weintraub in the elevator and immediately sensed that she knew who I was. I had created waves and was thus famous because I was infamous.

At first, only full professors and associates were eligible to teach graduate classes. When I became associate professor in 1965, I, too, became eligible, so another excuse had to be invented. All of a sudden I was told that only day session professors were eligible to teach in the graduate program. As it was a rule "across the board," I did not suspect discrimination.

The cat soon came out of the bag. I was at that time using Dr. Reid's desk and was sharing the office with a young, newly appointed psychologist who was teaching in evening session. We started chatting and I found out that he was also teaching in the graduate program. When I reported the matter, I was told that the man was "an exceptional case" and that it created financial difficulties for the evening session to replace evening faculty who were teaching graduate courses. This sounded very fishy to me, but I let it go.

By that time, I had been in evening session for many years and my reputation had grown so much that not only did I have an impressive number of philosophy majors, but more and more day session students were taking my courses at night. This was against the rules. Matriculated day session students had to take courses offered by day session professors. But there were two exceptions to the rule: first, if evening session programs offered a course that was not given during the day and, second, if the student had a "conflict" and therefore was "forced" to take an evening session course. Students are clever, and with time, more and more of them "created" conflicts to enable them to take my course.

Up until that time, apart from a course in philosophy required by the curriculum (usually logic), philosophy was a small appendix in the curriculum. I introduced new courses and, given the number of students I had at night, it became possible to offer philosophy as a major in the evening, which until that time was not possible because too few courses were offered to obtain the twenty-four credits required.

Whatever I introduced I always had the number of students required to give the course. To my colleagues' distress, from the time I was deported from the day session in 1954, I was the queen of the Philosophy Department in evening session, for I was the only full-time appointee at night. In the course of three years, philosophy majors could take all twenty-four credits required with me.

This created concern and bitterness among my colleagues, who had thought I would be eliminated by being banned from the daytime session. In fact philosophy in evening session, although still a fledging, was developing by leaps and bounds. I had risen from the ashes of defeat. It was urgent to find someone to counterbalance my nefarious influence over philosophy majors in evening session. A solution had to be found. I heard through the grapevine that it was being said that students in evening session were not presented a healthy variety of point of views. Philosophy majors were "forced" to take most of their courses with me. Once again, when Hunter was not in session (January) there was an emergency meeting, announcing that another tenured position was open in philosophy in evening session. (Surprisingly, the Philosophy Department got a new tenured position at a time when other much larger departments were competing for it.) I was on the Personnel and Budget committee and therefore entitled to vote. My colleagues knew that I was scheduled to give a lecture in Arizona, and the meeting was called knowing that I could not give my vote.

The man elected to the new tenured position was a

recent graduate from Columbia, who had been working in business, and as far as I know, had never taught. His name was Charles Sherover. He was over forty, and within three years he had his tenure without any difficulty. He was a passionate Kantian, and tried to convince his students that philosophy had, up until the eighteenth century, lived in the illusion that man's mind could know reality. Professor Sherover was not particularly eloquent, but he knew his subject.

Students love to pit one professor against another. When I once brought up the problem of the objectivity of truth and man's dignity to be able to know what is, a student raised her hand, and said that Professor Sherover had challenged this view. I refuted it as best I could. But it was not the end of the story. The same student related to me that she told Sherover that I had in turn countered his view. He responded, "Professor Jourdain, Professor Jourdain? Looking up to the ceiling, he "seemed" to make an effort to recall who I could possibly be. Then, as if he suddenly remembered, he said, "oh yes, you mean the nice French lady?" That was his way of "refuting" the objectivity of truth. Unwittingly, he had paid me a compliment, for there were not very many "ladies" in the city system. All this was cleverly calculated to protect students from intellectual "narrowness."

At any rate, he fulfilled the "mission" of "reestablishing" some sort of balance in the philosophy department in evening session. We did not see each other much, but got along well enough. He was not a radical leftist, and that, I must say, was refreshing.

CHAPTER 18

In 1961 the department held its first election, which at Hunter College occurred every third year. Since philosophy had become independent from psychology, Professor Clapp had been serving as interim chair; he therefore assumed he had the right to retain that position. When asked my opinion, I made clear I thought it was time for a change. There was no animosity in my answer (he was one of the two professors who lobbied Shuster to cancel my tenure track appointment in the day session back in 1953), but I was increasingly convinced that his behavior manifested serious psychological problems. He was an unhappy man who took out his frustrations on other people. A good chair needs self-control, some elementary fairness, and a friendly relationship with the various characters and temperaments making up a department—all of which he lacked, in my opinion. My colleagues told me that they too had decided against the interim, because they too had serious reservations about his capacity of be head of the department.

So who should be chosen? I had no interest in the post, even though being chair is probably the fastest way to promotion. Not only was I deeply convinced that I belonged in the classroom, but I intensely disliked administrative work, and probably would have done it very badly. I proposed Professor Wyschogrod, but he was reluctant and pointed out that being an orthodox Jew would make it difficult for him to attend the Friday afternoon Faculty Council (now replaced by the Hunter College Senate), which usually lasted after sundown.

John Meng, who had become president of Hunter in 1960, was informed there was to be trouble, and the department's voting professors were told to meet with him for the election. This meeting was one of the many painful moments of my life. The interim chair was so convinced he would be elected that he was especially friendly. When the ballots were read and he did not get a single vote, except probably his own, he practically had a heart attack, looking distracted, incredulous, and so resentful that he made all of us feel "guilty."

Professor Bryar, whom George Shuster had chosen to fill the tenured position to which I had been elected and then deprived in 1954, was as a Catholic, terribly anxious not to share my fate. He had prudently kept a very low profile on crucial issues, such as the objectivity of truth, and was finally elected as a minus malum. I knew that he was not made of the stuff needed to be chairman, but as Wyschogrod, who was my choice had turned it down, I had practically no choice left. The Communist, Professor Somerville was out of the question.

One reason Professor Clapp was so upset when he was not elected chairman in 1961 was that he feared that his textbook would no longer be used, and an important source of income would vanish. But Professor Bryar, wishing to prove his good will and desire to have peace in the department, announced that the textbook would be kept. The book was sold until philosophy was eliminated from the core curriculum.

That Professor Clapp was not elected caused quite a scandal in the college. Even though there was no reason to question the legality of the election, many thought and said that our interim had been betrayed, that he had a "moral" right to be elected, and that the whole affair was disgusting. One thing was certain: from the very beginning the new chair would not have an easy time. In fact, the stress was so acute that within a few months Professor Bryar had lost some twenty pounds. Everything he proposed was systematically opposed, ridiculed, or torpedoed. He had the sentimental idea that he was going to win his adversaries by fairness, kindness and patience.[*]

Although probably the hardest-working chairman I ever had in my career, with the very best intentions and boundless goodwill, this was the sort of person who had little contact with "real" life. He was an "intellectual" romantic. Alas, he was to learn through bitter experiences that he was living in a world of wishful thinking. He was soon to discover how shamefully illiberal liberals can be. The chairmanship was, for him, a long, drawn-out form of torture; for us, it was a total failure. It is a wonder he did not have a breakdown, considering the boundless enthusiasm and devotion with which he had started the job.

On the one hand, I am grateful to Professor Bryar. I finally became associate professor in January 1965, after eighteen years of successful teaching, under his chairmanship. On the other hand, his time as chairman was univer-

---

[*] I fear that he would have shared the view that one could "win" Hitler by fairness (as Austrian Chancellor Schuschnigg had thought) or that Russian Communists would treat the West with equity if only we could succeed in convincing them of our benevolence.

sally regarded as a failure. Everyone was displeased with
his performance, even those who had elected him *faute de
mieux* (for lack of anything better).

Clever as he was, Somerville immediately felt that he
could easily get into the good graces of the liberal Professor Bryar, and he succeeded. The chairman was so naive,
so out-of-touch with reality, and so convinced that by
sheer goodwill he could unify the department that he
was bound to become the prey of a superbly trained man,
who knew all the "techniques." When I came to Hunter
around four o'clock in the afternoon, I would find them
closeted together, engaged in deep conversations. The chair
was convinced that one of the important things he could
accomplish was to enter into this sort of "philosophical
dialogue" with a Marxist, infinitely cleverer than he was.

While taking the job terribly seriously as if it were a
sacred office, Professor Bryar had no judgment, constantly
called meaningless faculty meetings (even one on Sunday!)
that were nothing but a waste of time: fighting, bickering,
unproductive. Clapp, who had not been elected, had only
one aim: to prove the new chairman to be failure, which
turned out to be the case. He clearly enjoyed seeking
"sweet revenge." These meetings were not only meaningless,
but to me, sheer torture. Two professors, Clapp and Bryar,
were addicted to smoking but would not even allow me
to open the window of the small office where departmental meetings were held. Once I asked if they would mind
if I opened the window, and I was told that I was "selfish."
I usually left with a splitting headache, and then I had to
teach until ten o'clock at night.

At the end of one of these hopelessly fruitless meetings,

Professor Somerville left with me, saying that he was disgusted by the heavy smoking. He clearly viewed my colleagues as "decadent products of capitalism." I had the matchless stupidity of saying that I was allergic to smoke. At our next meeting, he lit a cigarette, turned to me, and said, "I have not smoked for a long time, but it does relieve tension."

How upsetting for me it was to have to listen at faculty meetings to the perorations of the ex-Catholic, Professor Somerville. He influenced Professor Bryar, who was the perfect incarnation of a "liberal liberal." Under Somerville's influence, Bryar tried to convince me that the "Church has now finally moved to the left (*apertura a sinistra*), and any faithful Catholic should follow her lead. Somerville expressed his conviction in a letter to the New York Times, claiming that he left the Church when he discovered that it "was not a Church of love," in contrast to the work of Lenin and Stalin, which were based on love for the people. I wish that Solzhenitsyn could have heard these words, he who had a taste of the "love" prevalent in Gulags! How in the world had I landed in a world so radically foreign to me: secularism, relativism, and communism?

We were sorely fractured. The former interim chair, Professor Clapp, for his part, was so bitter that he and Rosenthal formed a systematic opposition. When the new chair attempted, that fall semester, to appoint a friend of his to the department, he turned to me as someone he assumed would be supportive.

Unfortunately, the candidate's only "merit" was to publish an impressive number of articles "For a Free Algeria." I was not involved in the Algerian problem, one way or the other, but I personally objected when the classroom was used, as was often the case, as a platform for political views. To be pro "free Algeria" was, to my mind, no remarkable qualification for teaching philosophy.

I told the chair that, in good conscience, I could not vote for someone whose main interest was political. Professor Bryar was thunderstruck. He had been so absolutely convinced that I was going to follow his lead and all of a sudden here I was, refusing to endorse his candidate. Neither did the other professors he had supposed to be in his camp, so he had to acknowledge defeat and in his disappointment told me that I had "committed a grave sin." That was his Christmas gift to me.

In the meantime, Professor Bryar was working hard to create an ideal department of philosophy. One decision that he made toward creating peace was to inform me that because he and I were both Catholics, it would be better and wiser that I should not teach ethics and he had given the course to an adjunct. I was to teach logic, for ethics was "controversial," while logic was not. I objected: not only was ethics the field in which I had done the most work, collaborating with Dietrich von Hildebrand on the book True Morality and Its Counterfeits, but my course on ethics was highly successful and attracted a large number of students. I explained to him that my teaching ethics had nothing to do with being Roman Catholic; the natural moral law was available to everyone of goodwill. But he was adamant and I lost the course for a while. It is the privilege of the chair to decide who teaches what: I had no choice but to comply.

Bryar was unduly impressed by the academic world, and approached it as if it were a "sacred" enclosure. I could not share these views. Much as I rejoice over true greatness (I hope that I can say with Kierkegaard that "I have always been conservative in this respect, and have found joy in paying to the eminent and distinguished the deference, awe, and admiration which are due to them."*) I insisted upon making a sharp distinction between "famous" and "great." Teaching at a "prestigious" academic institution taught me that some "famous" people are not necessarily great, and that it is quite conceivable that some "great" person is not famous, even though it is quite likely that he will become so after his death. Alfieri had a point when he wrote, "*Sei vil o grande; mori, lo saprai*" ("Whether great or mediocre; in death, it will be known").

So I gave unconditional support when I thought I could and opposed what I must. After Bryar's chairmanship in 1965 and until his early death in 1979, he was shamefully treated and systematically excluded from important committee work. He had become a pariah and very often he would only get his vote and my own. He took this long, drawn-out defeat with great dignity and when a vicious cancer attacked him, carried his cross with admirable courage and nobility.

---

* Point of View, p. 51.

CHAPTER 19

I kept my first office for quite a few years, sharing it with two psychologists. Once again, I had a chance of observing that women, if they are not amazons, are ill-equipped at defending themselves. Trained to be friendly and polite, they are inevitably the victims of ruthlessness, and of the "superiority complex" of some machos—usually very mediocre representatives of the strong sex. Women, at times, are treated shamefully. When I entered my office, one of the psychologists, a day session professor, who chose to also teach at night, had his feet on my desk. When I came into the room, he removed them without an apology but as soon as I showed signs of going, he put his feet up again. I did not protest. My background had ill-prepared me to deal with such rudeness.

I vividly recall another incident which occurred when the Psychology Department insisted they could no longer house my filing cabinet. The office already contained three desks and the cabinet of another professor who became very upset that a second file would ruin "the aesthetics" of the place.

A couple of days later, he came to me radiantly and said, "I have found a place for your file cabinet." He took me all the way down the corridor; then we took a right turn, then another right, and between two doors there was a place for a cabinet. "I shall arrange to have your file moved over here," he said. I never dared contradict the arrangement, but one can well imagine how convenient it is to have a filing cabinet so far away from one's office. Once again, my convent education had not effectively prepared me for this sort of rudeness.

A couple of weeks later, a second filing cabinet appeared in our office. When I remarked upon it, the professor who had objected to placing my file cabinet in our office sighed, "Alas, our other colleague has brought his filing cabinet down and it does not look nice, does it?" I stammered, "But I thought you didn't want another filing cabinet in this office?" He answered, "I knew he would not give in, so I let him have his way." (In reality, he did not dare to force him as he was black.) "I didn't even try to challenge his wishes, but I thought I could convince you."

During Professor Bryar's time as chair, Professor Wyschogrod (the colleague with whom I got along best) decided to give up his tenure and accepted a position as chairman at Baruch College. He was understandably disappointed over the unbearable climate of the Philosophy Department at Hunter and, being clear-sighted, was convinced that there was no chance of redressing a situation rooted in ill-will. He was right, but for me, it was a great loss. As I already mentioned, he was an orthodox Jew and had been a good colleague and we collaborated on many issues. I found myself, once again, totally isolated.

The question of replacing Professor Wyschogrod became a completely hopeless affair. I could not endorse many of the candidates proposed, and was suspicious of others. As to the people I myself recommended, they were eliminated in the first round. A recommendation from me was the kiss of death.

I doubt I would have survived without a quick wit. One time, I was teaching a course in evening session downtown. My topic was the hierarchy of being. When I said that man was a higher being than animals, one of my students raised his hand in protest. "I am a Zoology major," he told me, "and I can prove to you scientifically that there is no essential difference between a man and a pig." I told him that I would appreciate hearing his arguments. He became quite eloquent, and told me that the length of a pig's intestines and that of human being is identical. The brains of both have the same weight and he went into other interesting details. He truly knew something about pigs.

I asked him how long he had been going to evening session. "Seven years," he answered, "and I hope to graduate next year." "You mean to say that for seven years, you have curtailed your evening meal and gone home very late costing you sleep, and that after making all these sacrifices, you will graduate with the conviction that you are no better than a pig? Was it worth the effort? Peasants know better than that." The students roared.

Some of my students were real characters. I recall that early in my career I had a little elderly woman who never said a word. She sat in the first row, and as soon as took her seat, she took off her shoes and wiggled her toes.

Then I recall the older Jewish lady who took my course on Social Philosophy. I am sure she enjoyed what she heard, but her problem was that she was tired and struggled to keep awake. It was late and perhaps she worked during the day. One day, she lost the struggle and fell sound asleep, to wake up just as I was raising the following question: What is the relationship between the part and the whole?

I had explained that the relationship existing between a pebble and the rock from which it was chipped was very different from the one between an organ and the body in which it functioned. I used these differences to highlight the relationship existing between an individual and the state. My student had missed it all. As she was talkative, and loved to show that she was actively engaged in class discussions, she pointed her finger at me, making sure that the whole class was listening to her, and then said solemnly, "I would say that the whole is greater than a part."

I told her that I could not agree with her more but that her statement was tautological, and I explained what "tautological" meant. She seemed to be thinking profoundly and then said, as solemnly as before, "Professor Jourdain, you made a good point there."

CHAPTER 20

From 1957 on I had to do advising in the School of General Studies, that is, I had to be in my office three hours a week to see students who needed help or advice. I had in fact been advising all along, long before I was appointed to tenure track. Evening students were very much neglected, and I thought they deserved the same attention as day session students. It was time-consuming, but gave me the chance to get to know many students. I learned a great deal about their problems and their frustrations in evening session, and I did my best to help them.

It is incredible how much one can learn just by listening. I found out that most of them had to struggle against great difficulties to come to school. I had known this before, but there is a great difference between knowing something in theory and in practice. Very many of them were poor; most came from broken homes, or found themselves in tragic situations. Through countless hours of advising, I came to understand that my courses were able to offer some meaning and light in their lives. They were a beacon, encouraging my students to confront the problems of human existence. Most were desperately in search of what Victor Frankl calls "meaning." Many were threatened by despair. What a beautiful privilege to help them find hope in finding truth. It is difficult to express how fruitful these years were. I had more and more students, and made new friends.

I recall a severely disturbed student came to my class draped in a sort of white sheet and wearing huge, dark goggles. He developed a passion for philosophy. He once came to my office and showed me a letter he was addressing to a famous writer who was known to be homosexual, praising his physique and offering his services. He wanted my approval!

He came from a broken family, like so many others, and had probably endured wounds in his early youth from which he never recovered. My husband spoke to him many times with incredible gentleness and patience. We drove him to his home on the West Side of Manhattan many times, making a detour on our way to New Rochelle, where we lived then. I recall giving him a New Testament. For a while I hoped that he would overcome his difficulties, but alas, his symptoms returned and he also ended up in Bellevue hospital. One day, we learned that he had been arrested for running naked through the streets. I never heard from him again. When I think of such students, all I can do is pray for them and remember that God is infinitely merciful.

The evening session continued to labor under unequal treatment. One fine day, we received the news that the teaching load was to be reduced from fifteen to twelve hours per week. That was a significant change, and much as I enjoyed teaching, I would have welcomed a shorter schedule because of serious problems with my vocal cords. This new rule, however, applied only to day session professors. I believe it took some eighteen months for this inequity to be corrected.

Soon, the scenario repeated itself: the day session teaching schedule was dropped to nine hours. Evening session remained at twelve hours for months to come. The more salaries climbed, the less professors in day session had to work. One thing is certain; some professors spent so little time in the classroom that they never learned how to teach because teaching is learned only by practice.

∾

The New York neighborhood where my husband had been living since 1941, and in which we now made our home together, was terribly unsafe. A woman had been raped in the lobby of our building, theft was routine, and we had to put a grate over our kitchen window to protect ourselves. But the rent was cheap, and we had no other place to go. My husband worried, as I always came home after eleven at night. Providentially, a week after the rape, he received an invitation to teach as visiting professor at the College of New Rochelle. The nuns put a small house at our disposal, and we finally left 448 Central Park West in September 1963.

In 1964, in spite of the mess and tension in the department, I decided to apply for a sabbatical leave. I had been teaching for seventeen years, and now that I had had tenure for seven years, I was eligible for a sabbatical. Further, my beloved husband had suffered a heart attack while lecturing in Mexico early in 1964, and I was convinced that a year of peace and rest would do us much good. My husband's darling niece, Clotilde Brewster Peploe, was now mistress of the beautiful first floor of the house in Florence where my husband was born, and she generously put it at our disposal.

It was a magnificent year, perhaps the most peaceful and beautiful of my life, rich in spiritual, intellectual, and artistic experiences. We worked, we read, we listened to great music, and we traveled. My husband taught a course in Salzburg from November 1964 to January 1965, and we went to the Holy Land in the spring of 1965. On June 21, we had a private audience with Pope Paul VI in Rome. Hunter and its problems were temporarily forgotten.

But I had to return to the lion's den in the fall semester. Just before we returned, my sister, whose husband was teaching at Iona College in New Rochelle, found an apartment for us in which I have been living ever since. It was a Godsend because we had no place to go back to.

Nineteen sixty-five was another election year for the chair position in the Philosophy Department. The situation was hopeless. There was such hatred among the members of the department that there was no satisfactory solution. Shortly before my return, I was informed that the president herself (Professor Gambrell, temporarily named president) had taken over and was imposing a new chairman on the department, that is, someone who was not elected by the faculty, but forced upon them, because clearly they could not come to any agreement. This was exceptional, but legal.

The chairmanship was given to a young British man, who had received his PhD from Yale. He had been trained as a scientist but had then turned to philosophy. He had taught only six years, mostly science, and then began working at the Carnegie Foundation.

For the many years that I knew him, I could never convince myself that he had even the most modest "philosophical eros." His knowledge of Greek philosophy was limited to textbook information and he knew nothing at all about medieval philosophy. His philosophical hero was David Hume and his expertise was analytic philosophy and philosophy of science. He made it clear that the philosophy department was going to be given a totally different direction. Classical philosophy was out; positivism and analytic philosophy were in.

Surprisingly, there was relative peace in the department under his chairmanship, a relief after the nasty bickering of the previous few years. Still, rapid changes took place and beginners in the field were appointed with salaries higher than those given to long-standing professors. Of course, professors in general were for a long time underpaid.* I already mentioned that I had been advising in the School of General Studies for years, first on a volunteer basis, then as an appointment, but without any course reduction or compensation. The new chair advised me to resign and immediately appointed another colleague to take over, granting him a course reduction. Understanding the beauty and importance of teaching, I did not so much mind the injustice, but physically the strain had been great (I left home at two-thirty to meet students for advising, only to return home at eleven at night), and students continued to come to me all the same.

I had hoped the new chair might rectify some of these

---

* The situation at Catholic universities was scandalously even worse. My own husband earned $7,670.00 in 1957: the highest salary he ever made at Fordham. At 65, he was kept on the faculty, teaching half-time at half that pay.

departmental iniquities. When I met him in the fall of
1965, I told him that I had been excluded from giving graduate courses. He expressed surprise and promised to inves-
tigate. But when I saw him again, he explained that—for
some mysterious reason—it could not be done. A few years
later, however, at an International Philosophical Congress
held in Vienna in August 1968, I saw Professor Sherover
(a very recent appointee), and he told me that he had been
invited to teach a course at the Graduate Center in September. He had received his doctorate in 1963; I had received
mine in 1949. He had been at Hunter for just a few years;
I for twenty-one. I was associate professor; he was assistant
professor. Why this opposition to the "nice French lady"?

I decided to go to a higher authority and approached
the Dean of Humanities, taking with me some twenty or
twenty-five letters that students had written me throughout my career and which all testified to the quality of my
work in the classroom. I put them in an envelope to show
the dean, who was very friendly.

I asked him if it was true that evening session teachers
were excluded from the graduate program. Of course, it
was not so and he could think of several people from the
evening session who were teaching in the graduate program.
I then told him that since the start of graduate program
in 1960, I had been systematically excluded from teaching there on the grounds that I was in evening session, and
yet a new appointee to the department, an instructor, was
now teaching there while I was still being excluded. He was
clearly displeased and bluntly told our chair that I should
no longer be excluded from teaching graduate courses.

The dean had read the letters and had been impressed by them. But when the next day, I went to his secretary to retrieve them, she told me that, knowing nothing about it, she had thrown everything into the wastepaper basket. It was upsetting. I had had no time to make copies of these precious letters. They were all original and were now lost forever. I think it was only carelessness or absent-mindedness on the dean's part. I am convinced that he was shocked at the discrimination to which I had been subjected and he did his best to correct the situation.

In the meantime, our chair resigned his post, himself moving to the Graduate Center, and seeing to it that a colleague he had brought with him to Hunter became the next chair. The latter had obtained a full professorship without a hitch.

I recall another episode which must have taken place before I finally succeeded in being "permitted" to teach graduate courses. We had a Personnel and Budget Committee meeting. The chairman informed us that we needed another professor to teach graduate courses, and he recommended a man who was currently teaching at Columbia University. This was to lead to a regular appointment.

I had just come back from Washington, DC where my husband had been lecturing and I had met someone who gave me a copy of the October 1966 Congressional Record to read on the plane ride home. To my surprise I read in these pages that the professor who had been recommended for appointment at Hunter was one of the most active Marxists in the academic world. At first, I refused to believe that it was the same man. In his Curriculum

Vitae, he had simply presented himself as a Kantian scholar. I checked the documents again and, of course, it was the same individual.

I gave my copy of the Congressional Record to a friend who had access to the president, and the next thing that I heard was that Professor Gambrell (the interim president) had opposed the appointment. Apparently my friend had called up friends at Columbia and discovered that this professor was a primary organizer behind the university's 1968 revolution. Gambrell was a no-nonsense person and the decision against the Marxist was final, although he was appointed on a part-time basis to give graduate courses.

Finally, in 1970, I taught my first graduate course. However, the program was discontinued some three years later when the Graduate Center developed a PhD program that absorbed the MA program, which meant I was back to square one. All those who wished to take part in the PhD program were invited to do so, but down to the very last day of my career, I was excluded.

Also in 1970, after twenty-three years of waiting, I finally got my full professorship. I had the slowest promotion in the department. From the very beginning of my career, I faced two significant stumbling obstacles: I was a woman and (horror!) a Catholic. I am still both.

Being a woman had certainly not helped my case. When I began my career in 1947, it was still rare for a woman to teach philosophy. The women who had achieved high positions and important posts in those years knew how to fend for themselves and were talented, hard-working, conscientious, and ambitious. They were typical amazons.

After 1970, the position of women appointed to the faculty improved considerably and my female colleagues who joined the faculty twenty-two years after I did, received full professorships with ease.

But the real animus against me, I believe, was a strong, anti-Catholicism. Anti-Catholicism was rampant in the city university structure but it was very subtle and thus difficult to prove. One of my colleagues was a Rabbi, while another was a Protestant Minister. But if a Jesuit applied for a position, his Curriculum vitae would immediately be tossed into the wastepaper basket. Obviously, no one was stupid enough to preach anti-Catholicism openly, because doing so could bring on a lawsuit. So it was accomplished covertly. The university had no difficulty appointing orthodox Catholics to secretarial work or to fields such as business and possibly languages. But philosophy—a field in which what one holds has great consequence—was of special "concern."

CHAPTER 21

By way of a humorous interlude, a long career like mine provided plenty of occasions on which my students' compliments were not always complimentary.

Introduction to Philosophy was, until the student "revolution" in 1970, a mandatory course. This meant that it was taken by many students who had no interest whatsoever in metaphysical and ethical questions. They "suffered" through it.

Some of them became convinced however that, after all, philosophy was not just a subject to be endured. One day, I was struck by the fact that a male student sitting in the back of the room seemed to be fascinated by my course. It is a pleasant feeling when a student seems to enjoy a course. It is amazing how "sensitive" a teacher is to the response he or she is getting.

After the class, he came over to me, and said, "Professor Jourdain. I have fallen in love." I told him how much I rejoiced for him. "Oh! It's not a girl. I have fallen in love with psychoanalysis. I am so fascinated by it that I psychoanalyze everybody. Throughout your course, every time you make a statement, I try to figure out what the psychological reason is for your position. It's so entertaining that I wanted you to know how much I enjoy sitting in your class."

I had another, similar experience. Once again, a student started radiating while I was expounding the Platonic myth of the cave. I had tried to show, as vividly as I could, the overwhelming experience of the philosopher who goes from shadows to light, and then having found it, is willing to make the sacrifice to return into the dark den because he feels morally obliged to share the precious truth found with his former fellow prisoners.

After the class, as expected, he came to see me. He told me that he had enjoyed my class immensely. I was in for a surprise when he said, "When you dramatized the experience of the man who left the cave and perceived the sunlight for the first time, it suddenly became luminously clear to me that I should become an accountant."

I also recall a lovely, elderly woman, Mrs. Fishman, who took my courses with passion. She was a kind, attractive old lady, but she certainly was not a born philosopher. The very fact that what I said was over her head gave her a feeling of elation. She felt she was partaking, however imperfectly, in something great and noble.

One day, my mononucleosis prevented me from teaching. I wanted to go to school very badly, but as the fever was rising, my husband adamantly opposed it and suggested that he substitute for me. As most of my students did not know who he was (I never mentioned him in the classroom), they were initially surprised but soon realized that they were in for an intellectual treat. My elderly student "fell in love" with him, not so much because of the greatness of his mind, but mainly because of his warmth and kindness.

When I showed up again the next week, she rushed over to me, and asked, "How is the darling?" Dietrich von Hildebrand had made a conquest. She continued to take

courses with me and each time I corrected her final examination my heart was heavy because, hard as I tried to rate
her generously, "C" was the very best that I could do. One
day, she came to my office, sat down, and started crying, "I
love your courses so much, but I know I am not doing well.
I have only one consolation." She pulled out of her pocket-
book a dirty piece of paper and said to me, "Read this." It
was a note from her grandson who had written, "Grandma,
if you flunk that test, don't you care."

There was something touching in this concern of the
grandchild for his grandmother. It was so typically American, in the best sense of the term. When I was a child,
grandmothers did not go back to school in their old age
nor did they need to be consoled by their grandchildren.

CHAPTER 22

In January of 1970, the acting-president of Hunter resigned. The usual political battle was on. One of the candidates was an ex-nun who had married a Jewish man by the name of Wexler. She had an MA in mathematics, but to be president of a prestigious institution like Hunter, a PhD was required. Jacqueline Wexler had made a very strategic contact with the Mayor of New York, John Lindsay. He spread the news that this very talented woman could not be elected president of Hunter because she lacked that diploma. In no time, she was offered an honorary doctorate (I believe she received more than one). The mayor had used his powerful connections to get his protegee this precious credential.

The newly minted Dr. Wexler became president of Hunter in January, 1970. She had only been in charge of Hunter for a few months when revolution broke out in the college, on March 19, 1970. Columbia University had faced a similar student revolt in 1968, so it was only a matter of time before the infection spread to Hunter.

When I came to the college that fateful March afternoon, the students had taken over the elevators, doors were barricaded, and there was a wild mass of people blocking the main entrance and chanting slogans. A typical déjà vu of revolution.

A couple of days later, President Wexler announced that an emergency meeting would be held in the auditorium (March 22 or 23). I attended. Before she came on stage, someone who taught in day session grabbed the microphone and started shouting abuses, accusing the faculty of being fascists. I did not know him, but later found out that it was a professor from the Political Science Department, whose brother headed the Communist Party in the Ukraine. A few days later, this same professor spat in the dean's face and was suspended for a short while, only to be fully re-instated in the name of "free expression and openness to other cultures."

Dr. Wexler began by announcing, "We have decided to close the college to avoid bloodshed; we do not claim any inspiration, natural or supernatural." The use of "we" was redolent of Catholicism. It was a blunder. The "liberals" roared with laughter. A reference to the "supernatural" was truly inappropriate. She must have realized that she had blundered, and all of a sudden, out of the blue, she announced, "I wish you to know that I have not prayed a single rosary in five years." I was stunned, but above all grieved. Not only was it an absolutely irrelevant remark, but it was so obvious that she shared this totally inappropriate piece of information as a *captatio benevolentiae*. That she had abandoned a classical Catholic practice had no interest for anyone, but the fact that she publicized it was meant to show that although she was an ex-nun, she had become "broad-minded" and embraced a liberal outlook. It was sheer pandering.

There is no doubt that Jacqueline Wexler had an exceptionally hard time when she took the job at the beginning of 1970. Many people were opposed to having an ex-nun in such a position, even though she had given ample proofs that she had "liberated" herself from bigotry. Nevertheless, a nun is a nun, though she was now married to a Jew and there is no doubt that she had to be imposed from above in order to be accepted by the Hunter liberal community. It took her a while to convince them that she was a friend and an ally. Be that as it may, she was treated abominably. She received insults and one reactionary student said that she would gladly murder her and throw her body down the toilet. That was the language typical of the revolution-aries. Facing this awful situation, President Wexler showed courage; nuns do get very serious training and know how to swallow humiliations.

The room was papered with leftist slogans and I became convinced that it was not a "spontaneous" revolt, but something that had been carefully planned. Classes were suspended, but I decided to give mine all the same. I took a side entrance, and managed to climb to the seventh floor where my class was held. Unfortunately, my knee was giving me serious trouble again and I had already made arrangements—as soon as the semester was over—with a renowned surgeon in Switzerland to have another try at surgery to repair the damage from the first botched opera-tion. I was in constant pain. But the elevators were blocked and I had no choice but to take the stairs. I climbed those seven floors, and discovered that I was the only one teach-ing on the seventh floor.

On my way up, I happened to stop on the second floor, where the evening session mail boxes were located. All of a sudden, a large black man jumped out at me and accused me of being a "white fascist." I had never seen him before, but very much doubt that he was a student. I retorted, "If my color bothers you, I'd be willing to paint my face black." This was surely daring and even foolhardy on my part. The Dean of the School of General Studies happened to overhear my remark and gave me a sign to be more prudent. He had the kindness to send a policeman to accompany me to my classroom and to stand guard in front of my room.

To my joy quite a few of my students attended class, which I held as if nothing had happened. But soon after, a policeman informed me that I was no longer permitted to continue teaching. The place was unsafe. I truly could not see why the whole semester should be interrupted because of these irrational and uncontrolled outbursts. The rumor was that revolutionaries had started fires and the danger was too great. I was told that they had also brought live rats into the building, which they set loose in the corridors. Another rumor was that the revolutionaries had poured ammonia on the food in the cafeteria. Whether it was true or just a rumor to create panic, I never found out. I saw several of my students shouting in the crowd and I had the feeling that they were enjoying the heated atmosphere and the sensationalism more than anything else. There is nothing easier than to get a "crowd" to join an eloquent speaker shouting fashionable slogans.

It was an ugly and unpleasant time. The whole semester was severely affected by the revolution. The students were restless and finally everyone was given a passing grade without regular examination.

Some of my students were clearly not only "pink," but red. In the spring of 1970, I gave a course on ethics. A couple of students were trying to steer the discussion with a clear political agenda in mind. I resisted. They wanted me to condemn the Vietnam War. In contrast to several of my colleagues, I never engaged in politics in the classroom. At one point, when one of them declared that the USA was an evil country, and that Communist Russia was the one hope for suffering humanity, I made it clear that I could not endorse her views, and even, unwisely, hinted at the fact that she should move to "the workers' paradise." No one was forcing her to stay here, and she was entitled to try a better "way of life." She then told me that she had no money. I suggested that she go to the Russian Consulate. Surely they would be willing to help someone longing for freedom and justice.

This was one of the few occasions on which I violated my rule not to bring politics into the classroom, but I thought in that particular situation, I should say a few words. Tragic and horrible as the Vietnam War was, there are cases in which it is legitimate to fight to prevent a great evil, in this case to prevent Communism from enslaving more people. I also added a few words on the danger of falling prey to propaganda. Two students viciously challenged me. It was a most unpleasant class and both students were seething with rage.

A few days after this unpleasant incident, I saw the dean of the School of General Studies, who told me very kindly that he hoped I was not upset. "What should I be upset about?" I asked him. "Haven't you seen the student newspaper?" Of course I had not. If I can help it, I never read gossip sheets. But in it, there was an article written by the revolutionaries, dividing professors into four categories. I had the honor of being listed among the worst and most deplorable, and students were warned to keep away from my nefarious influence. I told the dean that it did not upset me in the least because I am quite insensitive to criticisms motivated by hatred and prejudice, but I take criticisms very seriously when they come from people whose judgment and fairness one respects.

As I said, all this happened as my knee was once again causing me pain. As soon as the semester was over, I left for Europe, went to the hospital where I was immobilized for some fifteen days, and then spent most of my summer on crutches.

I came back to Hunter in early September and found a letter from both the president and the dean forwarding to me a letter they had received from my revolutionary students. I was accused of having escaped before the end of the semester because I "was anxious to rush to my castle in Florence." I never took the trouble to inform the president that my "Florentine castle" was a hospital in Basel.

One of the positive results of the students' revolution was that the college introduced teacher evaluations. At the end of every semester, students were asked to rate their teachers. For me, it was regrettable that teacher evaluations were not introduced before. They would have deflated the criticisms of my detractors. I say this, quite conscious of the fact that these evaluations can also become abusive.

There are two main drawbacks to teacher evaluations. First, students who dislike a teacher for very subjective reasons (e.g., the teacher gave them a bad grade) can "pay him back." It has always amused me to see that in several of my very popular courses, where my evaluations were very high, there usually were one or two students who would give me the worst rating possible. Usually I had no difficulty in identifying him or her. There is another danger. When teachers are struggling for tenure and they know that their ratings can play a role in their appointment, they may yield to the temptation of giving students higher grades than they deserve as a captatio benevolentiae.

On the whole, however, it is a sound practice. One cannot rate a teacher according to one evaluation. Every teacher has from time to time "a bad class," but if one keeps examining them, it is striking that some teachers are recognized to be outstanding in their classroom performance, whereas others constantly performing poorly. Yet some well-connected ones do get tenure. They are no guarantee of objectivity, however. The city university system is too politically oriented. When a candidate is "wanted" for non-professional reasons, no attention is paid to his weak or bad evaluations. On the other hand, it is quite possible that a teacher with above-average evaluations would be denied tenure.

There were, however, unpleasant "reforms" as well. For example, restrooms reserved for the faculty were opened to students, as it was undemocratic to have privileged toilets. I found out, for the first time in my life, how morally filthy a restroom can be.

I only saw President Wexler once, namely at the very end of a gathering to celebrate the "holiday season" at the college in December 1970. When I first came to Hunter, there was a brief Christmas party shortly before the break. All faculty and students who cared to come would assemble in the auditorium. Then-president George Shuster, a

Catholic, stepped on the stage to say a few words. He had been appointed commissar in Bavaria from 1950 to 1951 and had just returned to the US. He told the students that as he had spent a year in Bavaria, he thought they would be interested to hear how Christmas was celebrated there.

"As you certainly know, the Bavarians are heavy beer drinkers; they can absorb a tremendous quantity of that liquid, but their way of celebrating Christmas is to double the quantity, already copious in Advent, so that when Christmas arrives, very few of them are steady on their legs." It was not edifying, and I was grateful when a Protestant professor, Dr. Davidson, gave a brief speech reminding the students of the meaning of Christmas.

Some years later, Christmas was celebrated together with Chanukah. When the ex-nun became president, no mention was made of either religious holiday by name. A party simply celebrating "the holidays" replaced it. I had only a few minutes to attend but thought it proper to make the acquaintance of my new president who had been in office for some twelve months by that time and whom I had never met.

When I got to the Armory on 66th Street, the party was almost over—that is, instead of having to wait in line to greet the president, I found her chatting with someone, alone in a corner. I waited for a moment, and then when the other person left, introduced myself. She was very friendly and made a remark hinting at the fact that it had been a difficult year but that, fortunately, things were now under control.

I told her that I thought some faculty members had a heavy responsibility for what had happened, as it was clear that some of them had worked actively toward launching the "spontaneous" revolution. Without giving me a chance to complete my sentence, she told me that she agreed with me completely. So I added, "When professors teach students day in and day out that there is no objective truth, no objective values, and that is it 'all up to oneself to decide,' what had happened last March is bound to follow."

"What," she exclaimed, "you believe in the objectivity of truth?" "Indeed I do," I retorted. "Well, there I must disagree violently. Everything is relative," she replied. I remarked that this very statement implied a claim to be absolutely true. She answered, "That is pure play on words, Professor Jourdain. It may impress your students in the classroom, but with me this sort of reasoning does not work." She proceeded, "I went through a very serious crisis and I came out victorious because I found out that everything is relative. Since then I am a much better person."

I remarked that to base a serious educational system on the relativity of all truth and all moral values was a very doubtful undertaking, and had little chance of success. "It is precisely my aim to prove that it does work," she answered. I had to rush back to my last class and so I took leave of the president. Some two weeks later, I received my full professorship, which had already been approved by the board in November, 1970. I never saw the Hunter College president again.

CHAPTER 23

It is hard to imagine my career, with all its failures, had I not been carried along by the beautiful response of my students. Of course, I experienced many incidents with students to which the only response could be tears—and many prayers. But I was also repeatedly amazed at how my defense of truth would open my students to God's grace. And I cannot repeat often enough that I never mentioned religion, much less, Roman Catholicism in my classroom. The conversions that came were simply the fruit of a deep and reverent pursuit of truth in my classroom.

Back in 1969, I was, as always, teaching Introduction to Philosophy, a course I considered important because it was devoted to shaking the foundations of relativism. The class was full as always, but I was struck by a young woman in her early twenties whose expression at my words was regularly one of disbelief, as if to say, "Professor Jourdain cannot possibly mean what she is saying." When I raised the question: What is truth? She raised her hand, and gave me, as expected, a purely relativistic answer. I thanked her for her prompt reply, telling her that she had given the response I expected, and that I would spend the rest of the semester challenging it. She was stunned.

This expression of "disbelief" is something that I had witnessed more than once during my teaching experience. How often did my students say to me, "I never heard this before," to which I would answer that to learn is to become acquainted with insights one has not had before. I had come to see that relativism is the one great obstacle to faith. Once this bastion is torn down, the rest follows. Man's longing for God is thereby "unleashed."

She was clearly very intelligent, did very well in the course, took more courses, and decided to become a philosophy major. One day, she asked me whether I would allow her father to sit in my classes. I was giving an Aesthetics course, one of the very rare graduate courses that I was finally permitted to give, and my student came into the room with a very attractive, elderly gentleman. He audited the entire semester with a nice, friendly smile on his face and at the course's end, thanked me for having allowed him to attend my class.

Once, during a chance meeting with my student, I remarked to her that her father was so much older than she. She answered, "Yes, imagine, my parents got married and had two children, a girl and then a boy. Then the marriage went sour, and they divorced. Several years later they remarried, and then I came. This is why my siblings are some twenty years older than me."

That was an interesting story but it did not surprise me. I had been at Hunter for so long that I had become pretty "resilient" in the face of such stories. The semester being over, my husband and I went to Europe, as we always did. He usually gave talks, and we had the opportunity to visit his family and mine.

When I came back in September, I learned from another dear student of mine, that her father had died very suddenly that summer and that, although a philosophy major, she would take a semester off. I managed to find her telephone number, and tried many times to reach her, always in vain. One night, quite late, I finally got her on the phone and gave her my most heartfelt condolences, telling her how sorry I was she had lost someone so dear to her.

She started sobbing, and told me, "Yes, it was a terrible loss for me. Moreover, when going through my father's letters, I made a very upsetting discovery. He is actually my grandfather. My 'sister,' with whom I've always had a very strained relationship, is my biological mother. My grandparents adopted me, and I have always known them as 'Dad and Mom.' Now that I know the truth, I am shattered and deeply upset."

The blow was severe but she regained her peace. I introduced her to my husband and one day she expressed her desire to become a Roman Catholic. She was officially Protestant and was, in fact, a bishop of some sect, even though she considered herself an atheist, having been selected because she had a lovely voice. My husband and I were the happy godparents.

Then this dear student dropped out of school, caring for her "mother" who had developed terminal brain cancer and would die in 1976. My husband, too, was very ill; his heart condition was giving me the greatest concern. I learned through another student that our goddaughter was engaged to a Jewish boy.

We were both worried that the faith of this "very young Catholic" would be jeopardized. Even though ailing, my husband urged me to get in touch with her immediately, while informing her that he was too weak to talk to her but that I would be happy to see her.

Once again, it was late at night when I reached her. She promised to come to New Rochelle the following Saturday. My husband was in his reclining chair in the living room and I received her in the den so that he wouldn't be disturbed. She came punctually, but ...with her fiancé. This made it impossible for me to talk to her as I had intended. Her young man was attractive but seemed very shy and ill at ease. She told me that both a priest and a rabbi would marry them in a few, short weeks.

Just before she left, she begged me to allow her to say good-bye to her godfather. She came to the living room, knelt in front of him, and he gave her a blessing. I do not think her fiancé accompanied her. It was typical of my husband that he was willing to receive a beloved friend, even when he was utterly reduced.

In the meantime, my husband's condition deteriorated rapidly. A procedure to install a pacemaker in early October had been unsuccessful and he went into heart failure and lost consciousness. He was revived but stayed in the hospital for several weeks before coming home in late October. On the night of December 30, his heart began to race. I called an ambulance and he was brought to Mount Vernon hospital. Our dear friend, Fr. Vincent Miceli, S. J. gave him last rites. It was clear to me that the end was near. He remained in the hospital until January 24, when his cardiologist finally told me to take him home. There was nothing further to be done for him.

My husband's final months and especially his last days remain with me as vividly today as if they were just yesterday. I have written a full account of his death, which I am not yet ready to publish, but I can say that his death was the culmination of an extraordinarily deep life of faith. After receiving his last Holy Communion, he prayed the Anima Christi. When he came to the words *"jube me, venire at te"*—"And bid me come unto Thee," he repeated them three times as if with a crescendo of urgency. His death was a final ardent act of faith. God called him around six in the morning on January 26, 1977.

Of course, my husband's death prevented me from attending my student's wedding. To my joy and surprise, she was back in my classroom the next month with her husband. Soon she told me radiantly that she was expecting a child in the month of October. I reminded her that October was the month in which her godfather was born—on Columbus Day, to be exact. "It would be lovely if your little one were born on that day." She promised to do her best. On October 10, the young father called me, "My wife apologizes: the baby came two days early." I spoke to the mother who had delivered the baby at home and asked when it would be baptized. She answered airily, "Oh, probably at Christmas time, when my "sister" will be visiting from Alaska."

I hoped she wasn't evading the issue but, in fact, a couple of days before Christmas, her husband called me to inform me that the little boy would be baptized and gave me the name of the parish. Though I was totally wrapped up in the Christmas rush, I told him that I would come. Unfortunately, as I drove to the church, there was a bad accident on the highway, and I was stuck on the road for a full hour. When I finally arrived, the baptismal party was leaving. I expressed my regret that I missed this great occasion.

The proud father suggested that he would take me back

to my car. On the way, I told him once again, what baptism meant for us Catholics, and it truly was a source of deep regret that I missed this sacred solemnity. To my amazement, he answered, "Don't worry, there will be another one soon." I was stunned. What could he possibly mean? "I would like to enter the Church. Would you agree to be my godmother?" I was overwhelmed by God's mercy. Both husband and wife would now be confided to my special loving prayers. The young man was baptized on Easter Saturday, 1978, at Corpus Christi Church in Manhattan.

Unfortunately soon afterwards, they moved to Rochester, New York so that he might complete his education (he was pursuing a PhD in musicology), although practically every year after that, they were back in New York for a couple of days to have another baby baptized. But we always remained in touch. God gave them seven children and I treasure every single letter that my former student has written me. Even though they were living in difficult circumstances, she radiated joy and peace. It was clear that the marriage was a happy one and that all the children were received as gifts from God. To finish a very beautiful story, my "old" student is now active in fighting for Catholic orthodoxy and has proved to have great writing talent to put at the service of God. Two of her children have had religious vocations, while, to date, four are happily married, having given their parents sixteen grandchildren.

CHAPTER 24

There is a conversion story I must describe, if only briefly. Even though it is less dramatic than some other conversions experienced, this one gave my husband and me special joy. This student's conversion after some forty years continues to awaken my gratitude.

I was teaching, as always, one section of Introduction to Philosophy. One evening, I had already begun teaching, when the door opened, and a tall student wearing glasses, entered the room, and found a seat in the last row. He never said a word, but when the class was over, he came to me and said, "I noticed that I came into the wrong classroom. I had registered for another section, and by mistake entered your classroom. But what you said aroused such interest in me that I shall go to the registrar, and see whether I can register for your course."

He succeeded and to my joy, seemed to drink happily every word I was saying. He never raised objections, never challenged the ideas I was developing. He gave me the impression of someone very thirsty and happily drinking the water given him. Soon afterwards he came to my office, where my husband stayed while I was teaching, and made his acquaintance. To meet Dietrich von Hildebrand was to most people an experience! He greeted everybody with such warmth that those meeting him were grateful. Indeed, he radiated Christian love and the joy of being a child of the Church.

In a way, it was the smoothest conversion I ever experienced at Hunter. He seemed to have no difficulty in accepting the Church's teaching. Like Nathaniel there was "no guile in him." He was Jewish, and came from a liberal family. Not long afterwards, on March 1, 1970, he was baptized. We became his happy godparents, but he continued to take my courses. I believe he took all the topics I was teaching. To this day, he remains a source of joy. His faith is very deep and has given him the strength to carry the crosses that God has placed on his shoulders. To understand that suffering has meaning is one of the greatest blessings of Faith. Once again, my response is one of immense gratitude that God has chosen me as an imperfect instrument to share His message to those who thirst for truth and justice.

One of the most amazing conversions I experienced took place just before Christmas 1975. The story begins in the fall semester of 1974. I was teaching a course on metaphysics. I had already started my lecture, when a man in his late twenties stepped into the classroom, dragging his feet. His hair was long and unwashed. He wore a broad-brimmed hat and his body language expressed despair.

The man dragged himself to the last row, collapsed in a chair, and instead of facing me, turned sideways, facing the wall. He remained immobile, mute as a sphinx. I was convinced that he was not listening to me. Though the sight was not inspiring, he was in no way disruptive, as other students have been.

This went on for several weeks. He never cut a single class, and the same scenario repeated itself class after class. His hair was still unwashed, he still wore the same old hat, and he still sat on the last row, facing the wall, ostentatiously showing me his total lack of interest. What could I do except give my course trying to forget that I had a very problematic student in front of me?

One day, I was discussing the hierarchy of substances, placing inanimate matter at the bottom of the scale, followed by plants, by lower animals, then mammals, and finally placing man on top of the hierarchy, intimating that there might be other beings higher than man. I explained that a piece of matter was a substance, but if cut in two, it became two separate, but smaller substances. Such realities cannot claim real individuality. When it came to plants that are living, however, we faced a much higher type of unity, a principle of unity. And yet, an expert botanist can separate one part of the plant, put it in another pot, and the one plant becomes two plants. When we come to higher animals, this is inconceivable. If we cut a dog in two, we do not get puppies.

Finally, I spoke about the greatness of man: the fact that he has a soul, that he is capable of knowing, willing, and loving. I highlighted the fact that at the very moment of conception, the totality of the new human person is already present, even though it is still undeveloped. To this very day, I do not know why I added, "This sheds light on the horror called abortion."

To my amazement, the student in the back of the classroom jumped up as if he had been stung by a hornet and started shouting at me, accusing me of imposing my ideas on others. I was stunned. He had never appeared to pay any attention to what I was saying. Another student joined the protest and, for a little while, there was bedlam in the classroom. I prayed and responded the best I could, with my heart beating violently, struck by the fact that the "corpse" was alive.

During the rest of the semester, however, he never said another word. His final examination was a disaster; he hardly wrote more than a few words. I should clearly have given him an "F" but, to my shame, I calculated that if I did so, he might have to take the course all over again and I felt I had had it. To have a mummy in front of me for forty-five hours is not inspirational!

At any rate, I was convinced that I would never see him again. I was mistaken.

The next semester, in the spring of 1975, he registered for two of my courses. His appearance had not changed—same long hair, same hat—but he was no longer sitting in the last row. He selected instead a seat in the middle of the classroom. He never said a word but now he faced me, rather than the wall. That was an improvement. One day, he missed class, which was unusual as he was always so faithful. When I left, an attractive young woman rushed after me and said, "Are you Professor Jourdain? My brother sent me to apologize for cutting class today. He had a minor accident, and will not be back for a while."

I wished him a speedy recovery but was amazed that he had thought it necessary to inform me why he was missing class. Students often cut class, and never apologize. He came back after a couple of weeks and when I met him in the hall, asked whether he was fully recovered. He said "yes," and that was all. His midterm was much better, though even with the best of will I could not give him more than a "C–", I wrote a note: "big improvement."

The next semester, the fall of 1975, he took two more courses with me. Now he sat in the front row and once raised his voice to say, "Some philosophers put their intelligence at the service of truth, like Plato. Some at the service of error, like Nietzsche." I was stunned, but said soberly, "this is a very valuable remark."

Then came one of the most amazing days of my life. My first course was Introduction to Philosophy, given in one classroom. Then came the two courses in another classroom. These were the two my "mute" new friend was taking. I had just ten minutes between classes and was always hoping to have a moment of respite to catch my breath and recollect myself a little.

When I came to my office, five students were standing in front of the door. He was the first, so I invited him to enter. It was just before Christmas 1975. As soon as I closed the door, he practically jumped on me, and screamed, "I want to go to confession. Please send me to a priest . . . but you understand, a real priest." I was so dumbfounded that I didn't know what to say. I thought that he'd lost his mind, and my heart was beating violently. He asked, "Aren't you a Roman Catholic?" "Yes, I am. What about you?" "I used to be, but I lost my faith in the seminary. But you know, last night I had an overwhelming experience. God exists. These are not empty words. He exists and I want to go to confession."

I have a poor memory for telephone numbers but

through God's grace, I suddenly remembered the phone number of our dear friend, Fr. Vincent Miceli, S. J. When I called him, I usually would get the message: "Father is out of town; leave your name. He will call you back." This time, however, he was on the line within seconds. I told him I had a student who wanted to go to confession and he said, "Tell him to come tomorrow morning at nine-thirty." My student was there a half-hour early and stayed in the confessional for two hours.

Later that day, Father Miceli called me and expressed his gratitude to God for having worked a miracle of grace. The young man had come from a devout Catholic family who thought he had a religious vocation. The Maryknolls in Chicago accepted him and within weeks had torpedoed his faith with their "new theology," and modern Biblical scholarship.

He fell into a state of despair, left the seminary, and started leading a wild life. He had reached a point of suicidal thoughts when God led him to my classes. After two hundred and thirty-five hours of teaching, God's grace hit him. He came back to the Church and to the sacraments. He wrote me a couple of letters in which he expressed his gratitude for the help that, through me, God had given him. He had read Transformation in Christ, and wrote that he was praying for my husband and me. His hungry soul had received the food it craved.

Fr. Miceli quipped, "God works miracles: a young man loses in faith in a seminary and finds it back at Hunter College."

The same day, just as I was giving my last class that ended at ten in the evening, another student who had truly given me a hard time during the four courses he took with me, caught up with me as I was leaving the classroom. "Professor Jourdain, this was my last class with you. After taking the final next month, I'm entering the Air Force. I just wanted to tell you that when I started taking your courses, I had kicked religion out of my life. Now I shall go back to Church for Christmas." He was echoing the note from one of my earliest students—when I was still teaching GIs—that had so encouraged me back in 1948.

That was one of the most beautiful days of my life. When I came home, my beloved husband who always rushed to the door as soon as he heard the elevator, immediately saw on my face how moved I was. I told him, word for word, what I had witnessed. I still see tears running down his face. He was radiant and said, "There is no greater joy than when a soul finds their way back to God." We had a beautiful Christmas together, our last. A year later he was a dying man.

CHAPTER 25

I had two knee operations in close succession and had to take another sick leave in the fall of 1971 to recover. Moreover, my husband, who had suffered a heart attack while lecturing in Mexico in 1964, still continued to lead an extremely active life, lecturing in several countries and writing one publication after another, became very ill. He caught pneumonia and the doctor warned me that the state of his heart was so bad that he could not guarantee that he would pull through.

Thanks to a very strong constitution, he recovered, but from 1971 until his death in 1977, I lived in a constant state of anxiety. In spite of this, he continued to work until about five weeks before his death. Forty-eight hours before God called him back to Himself, he was still dictating to me details of his 1940 flight in France.

These years were very hard. I was under constant tension and fear, knowing that sooner or later my husband would leave me. Even though I continued to teach with the same devotion, and gave my students the same amount of time, I no longer attended all meetings, something I had always done. I do not recall that previously I ever cut a meeting, even though most of them were deadly boring and constituted a sheer waste of time.

I was now a full professor. I had been at Hunter twenty-four years and the development of the department was such that I knew I had no influence whatsoever and no chance of playing a positive role in its decisions. I was excluded from all committees and even those who acted as if they were "friendly" to me, voted against me. I had been a black sheep from the start.

Despite all this, my teaching gave me more and more joy as time went by. I had learned a lot, and except for a few individual troublesome students, there was not only peace in the classroom, but an atmosphere of intellectual excitement that was a pleasure to behold. Down to the last day of my career, I have had students who opposed whatever I said, but they were a relatively small, if sometimes vociferous, minority. The overwhelming majority of students were responsive to my teaching, as it was clearly shown in the evaluations I received from them.

Shortly after my husband's death in 1977, I was teaching Introduction to Philosophy and had a student in my class who was clearly talented. She turned in an outstanding exam and, as always, I was hoping she would take more courses in a field in which she clearly had a talent.

In the fall of that year, however, her name did not appear on my roster. I was disappointed because at the end of the semester, she had profusely thanked me for the course. I had been struck by the fact that several times, during class, she would blow her nose, and I did not suspect then that she was quietly crying. It baffled me, because Introduction to Philosophy was a very "objective" course.

After a month or so, practically out of breath, she ran into my office and, without any preliminary remark, said to me, "Professor Jourdain, I took your course last semester but I feared your influence and decided to avoid taking more classes with you. I turned to other professors for my philosophy credits. But the course I am now taking is awful. It depresses me so. I shall go back to your classes." She kept her word, became a philosophy major, and must have taken some seven courses with me.

One day, she asked to talk to me privately; I invited her to come to New Rochelle. She spoke for four straight hours. I didn't dare move or breathe for fear of interrupting. Her life had been tragic. She was the child of parents who were severe alcoholics. They loved their daughter but periodically went on binges and were found drunk in the gutter.

Several times when a little girl, she found herself all alone and then would ring the bell of a neighbor and ask them to feed her and take her in. They complied many times, but once the parents did not show up for ten days and the neighbors called the police. The girl, about eleven years old or so, was taken to a home for abandoned children. "It was hell," she told me.

She was on the brink of total despair, when the warm-hearted mother of one of her school friends, finding out what had happened, got her out of this "shelter" and offered to be her foster mother. She was a divorcee, had two daughters, and had married a man who was also divorced, and who also had two daughters. The place was not always peaceful and my student was often made to feel that "she did not belong there." But the foster mother must have been a noble and kind woman to whom she truly became attached.

At seventeen, she went her own way, working on a kibbutz in Israel, then going to Australia, and finally returning to the US. A couple of times, she tried to take her own life, once trying to cut her veins in the restroom at Grand Central Station. Then she landed in my classes and through God's grace, found her way to the Church.

When she told me of her interest in Roman Catholicism, I sent her for instruction to the priests of the Opus Dei who had a house just a block from Hunter. The Opus Dei community took her to Italy where she was baptized, received the Sacrament of Confirmation, and her first Holy Communion from His Holiness Pope John Paul II on Holy Saturday, 1980. After the ceremony, His Holiness gathered all the newly baptized into the Chapel of the Blessed Sacrament in St. Peter. He spoke a few words to each one of them. The Opus Dei people had told her that this was going to happen, and asked her to inform the Pope that she had received her instruction from Opus Dei priests in New York. But in her excitement, she forgot all about it, and when the Pope kindly questioned her, all she could think to say was, "I am a student of Dr. von Hildebrand." I had not told the Pope when I was privileged to see him in a private audience in January 1980 that I had a doctorate. Thinking that my student was referring to my husband, His Holiness said, "He is one of the very great thinkers of the twentieth century."

She went back to New York. Her (biological) parents, who by this time were divorced, knew nothing about her conversion. She saw them rarely, but one day, she decided to pay her father a visit.

She found him fuming and raging. He was reading the New York Post and saw, to his horror, a photograph of his daughter being baptized by the Pope. When my student returned to New York, the Opus Dei people had asked the paper whether they would be interested in printing a photograph of a New Yorker baptized by the Pope. They came over immediately and printed the photograph taken during this young woman's baptism.

Her father was particularly enraged at the fact that the article claimed that he was an atheist. She objected that it was accurate, for he did not believe in God. He then exclaimed, "Of course, but all the same I am a Lutheran!" Unfortunately for me, at the bottom of the article, there was a brief caption stating that she had been studying philosophy at Hunter College, had developed an interest in Catholicism, and went to Opus Dei for instruction.

My student wasn't the only one who paid dearly for that photograph. As the devil never sleeps, one of my colleagues saw the article, cut it out of the paper, and put it ostentatiously on the bulletin board of the Department of Philosophy. Once again, my colleagues had blatant "proof" that I was spreading Roman Catholicism in the classroom. I was not mentioned by name, but it was not difficult to guess who the culprit was. Thank God, I had my full professorship by then, and could no longer be harmed.

Another amazing conversion took place around the same time. I was giving the Introduction to Philosophy course. The class was full, and, as always, I spent several weeks debunking subjectivism and relativism. I knew by experience that this is the basis and foundation of any sound philosophical reasoning.

At one point, I declared, "I hope that I have now convinced you of the objectivity of truth." To my utter amazement, a male student in back of the room rose (which was unusual for Hunter, where, when students question you, they always remain seated) and said in a strong, clear voice, "Professor Jourdain, I object to your spreading Roman Catholicism in this classroom."

I perceived the viciousness of this remark. Many of my students could not possibly know that I was Roman Catholic and I had not said a single word about religion. He had clearly been "briefed." My heart was beating violently and I quickly prayed, "God, come to my help."

I caught my breath and said, as calmly as I could manage, "I'm afraid you have committed an anachronism." I purposely used a word that, I assumed, he would not understand. Reading puzzlement on his face, I asked, "Do you know what an anachronism is?" Of course, he did not. I then explained to him the meaning of the word and added, "All the arguments I have used to refute subjectivism and relativism were taken from Plato and Aristotle who were born respectively the fifth and the fourth century before Christ. That should take care of your objection."

There was a complete silence in the classroom. Everyone was watching the scene with fascination.

In the front row, there was a young woman who had struck me because I could feel that she was drinking in every word I said. She had a lovely, attractive face, and big blue eyes. She never said a word in the classroom, but gave me an outstanding exam. The next semester, she took my course on Plato. Once again, she gave me a flawless examination. I was hoping to have won her over and expected her to major in philosophy, but she disappeared from sight and I forgot about her.

A year or so later, in June, just as I was getting ready to drive to Hunter and proctor final examinations for four hours, a woman called me and said, "Maybe, you have forgotten me. I took two courses with you some time ago, and I urgently want to talk to you." I told her that I was about to leave for Hunter to administer exams and then I would be tied up with the correction of the tests, and leaving for Europe a couple of days later. I suggested that she try to see me in the fall.

She started crying and said, "No, I must see you immediately." I was puzzled but realized that she must need serious help, and I asked my friend, Mücki Solbrig, to proctor my first examination so that I would have time to speak to this young woman. Upon entering my office, she was waiting for me and I immediately recognized her as the student who had done outstanding work in two of my classes, the young woman with the lovely blue eyes.

"What can I do for you?" I asked. "Dr. Jourdain, I want to become a Roman Catholic." I was taken aback. That truly was the last thing that I had expected to hear. I asked, "How did this come about?" "After taking your classes . . ." "But, I never said a word about Roman Catholicism in my classroom. I taught philosophy, not religion." "I know," she answered. "But do you remember that one day a student accused you of spreading Roman Catholicism in Introduction to Philosophy?" "Of course, how could I forget?" "At that very moment, grace hit me. I was raised a Baptist with very strong anti-Catholic prejudices. I didn't know you were Roman Catholic, but I loved your course. When this man challenged you, I understood that what you were teaching was in harmony with Roman Catholicism, and I realized how prejudiced I had been. I then took a second course with you. I was sitting next to a girl who said to me, 'she teaches under her maiden name, but she is married to a famous man, Dietrich von Hildebrand, who has written many beautiful books.' I went to the library, read one of them, and now I am convinced. I want to become a Roman Catholic."

These are moments when one is overwhelmed by God's providence. He had chosen the nasty remark of a man who had been told to harm me and warn my students to be on their guard, "Be careful, she is trying to indoctrinate you." God used this nastiness to bring another of his little ones into the fold.

I noticed that she was wearing a ring. I asked her whether she was married. Yes, and she had two small boys. "What will your husband say about your interest in Roman Catholicism?" She started crying again and said, "He doesn't know anything about Roman Catholicism. His job is to sell birth control pills, and some of his clients are priests and nuns. But his opinion doesn't matter at this point. He wants to divorce me. Recently, he was offered a top-notch job in a big pharmaceutical company in California and told me that I was a satisfactory wife so long as he was a nobody but now that he had become a big shot, he needed someone who was more 'suitable.' On the other hand, he wants me to move to California so that his two boys will not be raised far away from him. We are leaving in a few days; this is why it was urgent for me to talk to you. Could you recommend a good priest in California to whom I can go to for instruction?" I was deeply moved. When I came home that night, I called Fr. Robert Bradley, S. J. who, I knew, had connections in California. He recommended a certain Fr. Sweeney in Santa Clara.

So, in time, my student entered the Church. In 1993, I was giving talks at Human Life International in Santa Clara. To my joy and surprise, I found out that the meeting was taking place in Fr. Sweeney's parish. I went over to the rectory, and asked him whether he had baptized a student of mine and gave him her name. He looked it up in his register, and there it was; she entered the Church in December of 1977.

God's overwhelming providence had scored another victory. She later made the acquaintance of dear friends of mine in California who told me that she was practicing faithfully. From time to time she wrote to me, and I had the joy of seeing her again in 1996, in Houston. Such gifts of God's grace make one forget many of the injustices one suffers. As a matter of fact, imperfectly as I accepted them, it was probably the small contribution that God asked of me to help a beloved soul come home.

CHAPTER 26

In December 1983, I officially announced that I was going to retire on September 1, 1984 and that I would already cease teaching in the spring of 1984 thanks to vacation time I had accumulated. I wanted to devote myself to my husband's legacy and could no longer combine this very absorbing work with a full-time teaching position. When I announced to my students that I was retiring, I could see disappointment on every face. I was deeply touched. They gave a party for me, showered me with gifts, and several of them asked whether I would not be willing to give a seminar in my home, to which I agreed and gave a special course through the spring of 1984. They even collected signatures for a petition to the department asking that I be invited back on an adjunct basis.

For years, I had been asking my chairman to let me teach a course on the philosophy of love, but every semester it was given to someone else. On one occasion it was assigned to a young man who had just been appointed and I was asked to sit in to review his performance. All he did was ask students to speak about their first sexual experiences, how young they had been, and so forth. As soon as the chairman discovered I was retiring, he gave me the course.

On registration night after just one hour, all forty-five seats were filled. Some students even asked if they could stand. As a result, every square inch of the classroom was packed. This was a topic on which I could be very eloquent, having worked closely with my husband on his philosophical magnum opus The Nature of Love, though obviously I left out the Catholic note. It was the only course in my long career at Hunter in which I never had a single interruption from a student.

I have a humorous memory of speaking about love of neighbor. When I mentioned that this form of love is already described in the Old Testament, one of my Jewish students, whom I liked very much, raised his hand. "What you say is correct," he said, "but for Jews the love of neighbor applies only to fellows Jews." "Thank you for this information," I said in my best deadpan.

Around the middle of the semester, I tried to escape during the break to catch my breath. A woman, probably her in her fifties, came running out of classroom, "I must speak to you urgently," she said. I invited her into my office where upon sitting down she started sobbing uncontrollably. When she could finally speak, she said, "Today you spoke so beautifully about the love between man and woman. I had a horrible marriage. My husband recently died. I can't tell you how liberated I felt when I buried him, but after listening to you, I now realized what I missed. Marriage is one of our greatest gifts in life, and yet mine was a mess."

Finally came the day of the very last class I ever gave at Hunter as a professor. Once again, this same student rushed after me. "I must talk to you." Once again, she sat down and started sobbing; she was absolutely shaking with emotion. I waited until she recovered, while trying to comfort her. "After taking your whole course on love, you have brought me to a much deeper level," she said. "I now realize deep down that I truly love my husband, yet now it is too late to tell him." Again, sobs. I was deeply moved. I said to her, "Love is a promise of eternity. As Gabriel Marcel says, to love someone is to say, 'thou shalt not die.' I assure you that you will still be given another chance to tell him of your love."

In 1980, Donna Shalala became president of Hunter College. She later became chancellor of the University of Madison, Wisconsin, before being appointed Secretary of Health and Human Services under Clinton. She introduced an award system, one for excellence in teaching, one for service to the college, and one for scholarly work, to be given during graduation ceremonies.

One day, one of the students brought me my mail from Hunter, which had accumulated for weeks. In it, I found a notice informing chairmen that they should soon nominate professors for the various awards that were going to be given at the graduation in May 1984. I was about to leave for New Hampshire, where I had been invited to lecture and hastily collected some updated information that I forwarded to my chairman. And then I forgot all about it. My chairman submitted my name and that of another colleague with high student evaluations for the excellence in teaching award.

I had been invited to appear on a TV show in Los Angeles that April and was preparing my trip when the phone rang. President Shalala's secretary asked to speak to Professor Jourdain. "The president of Hunter College wishes to speak with you." And suddenly, there was President Shalala on the phone, informing me that I had been granted the award for excellence in teaching, and was going to receive this award on May 30 at Madison Square Garden. I had already made plans to go to Europe, but hastily changed them. Needless to say, I was stunned. Close to thirty-seven years of hard work and discrimination whirled through my head: the persecutions, the calumnies, the spying, the delayed promotions to which I had been subjected, and here I found myself on the podium of Madison Square Garden with the "authorities," honored as an outstanding teacher who had been selected from a faculty of hundreds of other professors.

The experience itself, however, was surreal. Before the ceremony started, the entire faculty was assembled in a large hall where they donned their caps and gowns. I was standing by a door and suddenly someone nudged me and said, "Look, there's Shirley MacLaine." "Who is she, anyway?" I muttered. The professor looked at me with an expression of pity mixed with disbelief, but before she could enlighten me, my name was called and I had to join the procession of big brass and entered the immense auditorium. Some five thousand students were graduating.

There were three honorary doctorates being given that day. One went to an alumnus of Hunter who had done some outstanding work in biology. Another was granted to a black woman from South Africa who had been a close associate of Biko before his death, and the third one was given to that mysterious woman, Shirley MacLaine. I never did figure out what she had done to deserve the honor, but the speeches that day had a strong political tone, with one predicting the victory of feminism and that a woman would soon become vice president of the United States.

Bella Abzug was sitting two chairs down from me and she also said a few words. It was not my cup of tea.

The professor who was honored for service was Vera A. Roberts, and the award for scholarship was given to Wendell Johnson, no doubt a very worthy scholar, of whom there are some at the city university.

The president of the student body gave an unpalatable speech about freedom and free love. When I left Madison Square Garden my dear friend, Sheila Flanigan, whom I had invited as my guest, embraced me and said, "Lily, I knew that you have had a hard time at Hunter, but after the speeches I heard tonight, I have become fully conscious of how arduous your task must have been." Yes, universities can be nurseries of evil philosophies and hotbeds of revolutions.

A FINAL REFLECTION

My long struggle uphill was over and now it was suddenly crowned with a victory. I looked back upon my professional life and asked myself: had I known the persecutions that I would suffer for years, would I have accepted the job? The answer is that God, in His Goodness shows us only a small part of the path He is leading us on; had I seen the whole trajectory at once, the coward sleeping in me would have refused the challenge. However, if I had to live all over again, would I change my approach to teaching, as so often I was "commanded" to do?

Without hesitation, I can answer, "no." While I am convinced that I could have done lots of things better and that I made plenty of mistakes in the classroom, "my approach to teaching" has been an uncompromising devotion to truth, a passionate desire to share with others what I myself have received, an absolute refusal to compromise for the sake of worldly advantages. I could not join the bandwagon of those who reflect the "spirit of the times" or "what the age demands."

It is true that this systematic refusal "to play the game" and join hands with those who view teaching as a means of earning money (and it can be lucrative if one is clever), explains the fact that I was a professional failure. But if the "successful" professors only knew the joy I have experienced in the classroom, if they could only suspect how rich and fruitful my teaching has been, how many dear friends I have made, they would perhaps see that I have chosen the better part.

How I wish I could convince the administration of a school like Hunter that there is a tremendous need for teachers who courageously stand up for the objectivity of truth. There are things which do not change, which have an absolute and transcendent validity, and which every person has the right to know. Religiously, morally, humanly, and politically our great nation can only hope to survive if it stands firmly on the ground of truth and gives its children the bread for which they hunger. This is the great task of education.

In spite of all the mistakes I might have made, I believe I can honestly say that I never compromised what I knew to be true for the sake of worldly advantages. So, even though I am a failure, I am a most successful and happy one.

Saint Benedict Press publishes books, Bibles, and multimedia that explore and defend the Catholic intellectual tradition. Our mission is to present the truths of the Catholic faith in an attractive and accessible manner.

Founded in 2006, our name pays homage to the guiding influence of the Rule of Saint Benedict and the Benedictine monks of Belmont Abbey, just a short distance from our headquarters in Charlotte, NC.

Saint Benedict Press publishes under several imprints. Our TAN Books imprint (TANBooks.com), publishes over 500 titles in theology, spirituality, devotions, Church doctrine, history, and the Lives of the Saints. Our Catholic Courses imprint (CatholicCourses.com) publishes audio and video lectures from the world's best professors in Theology, Philosophy, Scripture, Literature and more.

For a free catalog, visit us online at
SaintBenedictPress.com

Or call us toll-free at
(800) 437-5876

CPSIA information can be obtained
at www.ICGtesting.com
Printed in the USA
LVHW082338250422
717209LV00017B/176/J